MW00618313

BOISE CLIMBS

For my son Eagan John Epeldi

In memory of my sister Theresa Bacus

Michael Stoger climbs into the sunset on his route, **Fotzhobel (5.12c)**.

BOISE CLIMBS
Third Edition

A guide to rock climbing in the Boise area

By Sandy Epeldi

Foreword by Pete Takeda

Boise Climbs
Third Edition
© 2003 Sandy Epeldi

ISBN 0-9743038-1-X

All of the information in this book was compiled prior to June, 2003.

For further information visit: **www.boiseclimbs.com**

Photo above and on the cover: Suzanne Lee on **Beta Junkie (5.10c)**
Photographed by John Laughlin, 2002

Back cover photo: **Max V (5.11b)**
Photographed by John Laughlin, 2000; Collaged by Sandy Epeldi

Acknowledgements

Thanks to the following people for their assistance and contributions:

Jay Aguinaga, Bob Allen, Kirk Anderson, Bruce Bedell, Scott Bernstrom, Bob Boyles, David Casey, Charlie Crist, Jason Cronk, Scott Dewalt, Jesse Edmundson, Brian Fedigan, Frank Florence, Steve Fransen, Matt Fritz, Preston Glaisyer, Flora Green, Kip Leon Guerrero, Tom Harper, Rob Hart, Mathew Henderson, Bob Jahn, Taylor Jenson, Jeremy Johnson, Phil Johnson, Shawn Johnson, Jeff Landers, John Laughlin, John Lavey, Cade Lloyd, Isaac Madarieta, Mike McClure, Tom McLeod, Todd Meier, Bob Meyers, Nick Meyers, John Odle, Curtis Olson, Chris Parker, Pete Pollard, Nick Ray, Steve Riccio, Dan Smith, Georgeanne Smith, Jeff Smith, Jamey Sproull, Michael Stoger, Pete Takeda, Tedd Thompson, Scott Urban, Mike Weber, Steve Young

A special thanks to my wife Sarah Brandenberger for her patience and support

Foreword

For me climbing is a continuum of experiences. The continuum started over 20 years ago on the boulders of the Table Rock Quarry. Today, at the beginning of the new millennium, I'm just starting to take on big league mountains in Canada, the Alaska Range and the Himalayas. For myself and a few other scrappy malcontents from Boise High, the boulders of Warm Springs Mesa and Table Rock yielded an ideal mix of psuedo-athletic movement and angst ridden escapism. The first climbing I ever did was the Crack Traverse on Space Mountain. Turning the arête above the jagged landing left me a shaken wreck for a day. After that moment, I was hooked.

Climbing stood equal footing with huffing moldy 'lumbo and cranking skull splitting punk rock. Bouldering led to toproping. Toproping finally led to shaky lead climbing in the early-80's pre-bolt days at the Black Cliffs. Our early gear would make the modern climber gag—waterski ropes, home slung machine nuts, and Converse All-Stars. My friend Cade Lloyd even trusted his life to a set of funky tapered metal wedges pilfered from a print shop.

When it came to belaying, rope work, and gear placement, we sucked. We owned gear, but without instruction, it was just enough to get us into trouble. Cade took a near-deck zipper fall aiding the Propeller when he neglected to place a directional piece at the base. Besides being ignorant we were slow learners—I took the same fall the very next day when I also failed to place a directional. The next year I dropped the second to the deck after leading a then-harrowing Doug Scott crack. I led the route, but didn't know how to belay properly.

We survived our youth and went on to establish routes, some of Boise's first 5.12's. Some of us left to climb in places like Yosemite, Smith Rocks, and beyond. I went on to climb trad routes, sport climbs, walls, ice and now spend more than my fair share of time sucking thin air in the great ranges. Though I've seen the lodgepoles dwindle like toothpicks from high on El Cap and gasped like a fish in the thin Himalayan air, I'll never forget where it all started—ten feet up, wide eyed with fear, gunning for the next hold in a quarry in Boise.

Pete Takeda
November, 2002
Boulder, Colorado

photo by Cade Lloyd, circa 1982

Pete Takeda, early in the continuum, on the former Quarry classic, **AC DC (5.11a)**.

Contents

Contents

Contents

Boise Region Overview

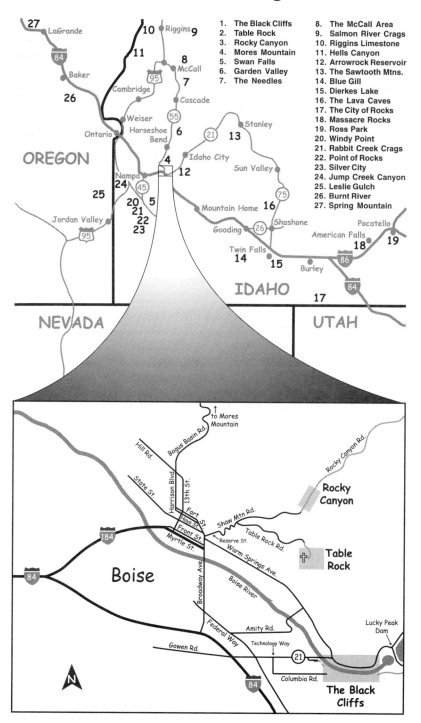

1. The Black Cliffs
2. Table Rock
3. Rocky Canyon
4. Mores Mountain
5. Swan Falls
6. Garden Valley
7. The Needles
8. The McCall Area
9. Salmon River Crags
10. Riggins Limestone
11. Hells Canyon
12. Arrowrock Reservoir
13. The Sawtooth Mtns.
14. Blue Gill
15. Dierkes Lake
16. The Lava Caves
17. The City of Rocks
18. Massacre Rocks
19. Ross Park
20. Windy Point
21. Rabbit Creek Crags
22. Point of Rocks
23. Silver City
24. Jump Creek Canyon
25. Leslie Gulch
26. Burnt River
27. Spring Mountain

Introduction

ABOUT THIS BOOK

This book details rock climbing within the greater Boise area. The main areas described are the Black Cliffs and Table Rock. These two crags, boasting hundreds of routes within fifteen minutes of downtown, are the focal point of rock climbing activity in the Boise Valley. Other areas included are Rocky Canyon, Mores Mountain and Swan Falls. These various crags offer a diversity of rock types and climbing experiences within a stone's throw of Boise.

In 1994, I published the first edition of this book and since that time climbing in the Boise area has seen some profound changes. Literally hundreds of new routes have been established, whole new crags have been developed and the sport has boomed in popularity. The Black Cliffs, in particular, have seen unprecedented route development with roughly one hundred new sport routes installed, many new crack climbs established, and whole new cliff bands developed. In other corners of the Boise area, new climbing sites have sprouted up, such as the top-notch bouldering area, Swan Falls and the granite sport crag, Mores Mountain.

One of the goals of this book is to familiarize Boise climbers with the myriad of climbing opportunities available to them. In addition to the hundreds of routes that are practically within city limits, Boise is strategically located for short road trips to other climbing sites. There are dozens of places to climb in the region ranging from tiny backwater crags to major climbing areas that sport hundreds of routes. I have included some general information for those of you looking to explore beyond the Black Cliffs and Table Rock. There are thousands of routes throughout the Boise region, so stop reading this drivel and go out and climb!

BOISE HISTORY

People have lived in the Boise region for well over 10,000 years. The area's earliest inhabitants were hearty souls who hunted big game such as elephants, camels and bison. The climate they endured was much colder and wetter than today's and was probably lousy for sport climbing. Throughout the centuries, the regional peoples were subjected to major changes in the climate as well as shifts in the local flora and fauna. This led to many cultural modifications as the area's inhabitants adapted, moved about or were replaced by new inhabitants. Eventually the Northern Shoshone culture emerged in southern Idaho with the Boise Shoshone band based in the Boise Valley.

For many centuries, the Boise Shoshone traveled with the seasons in search of food. During the summer, plentiful salmon runs on the Boise River provided sustenance and attracted neighboring tribes for festivals and trade. The area's surrounding hills and plains provided a variety of wild game—ranging from rock chucks to elk. The former was considered a delicacy and could have been a precursor to power bars. During the spring, journeys were made to Camas Prairie to gather camas root, which was a highly valued food source. After horses were acquired, fall journeys were made to the Great Plains for buffalo hunts. The Boise Shoshone and their predecessors also frequented the crags we now climb. Keen-eyed boulderers might notice clues to this past.

By the early 1800s, fur trappers were trickling into the Boise region. Donald McKenzie, a renowned explorer and trapper, discovered beaver rich country in the region and in 1819 held a trapper's rendezvous in the Boise Valley. This rendezvous was part of the Boise Shoshones' annual salmon festival and was probably as wild and woolly as a modern day base camp shindig with the infamous Boise climber, Tedd Thompson. The Boise Shoshone regarded beaver hunting as an absurd occupation that no one of reasonable intelligence would pursue. This same sentiment could easily apply to the pursuits of modern rock climbers.

In 1833, the military explorer Captain Bonneville arrived in the Boise Valley after an arduous journey across the barren Snake River Plain. He and his men were elated when they crested a hill and saw the tree lined Boise River below. In his excitement Bonneville uttered, "Les bois, les bois! Voyes les bois!" (The woods, the woods! See the woods!). These historic words ricocheted off the Black Cliffs and implanted a name on the river and valley below. Earlier names for the river included the Shoshone name, "Wihinast" or "Boiling Rapidly", "Reed River", in honor of fur trapper John Reed who had been murdered nearby, and "Skamnaugh", which was the name Donald McKenzie had applied in honor of a local Indian band.

From the early1840s through the 1860s, tens of thousands of emigrants traveled through the Boise Valley on the Oregon Trail. Many of these travelers made note in their journals of the valley and its wooded river. Some emigrants even mentioned the Black Cliffs and Table Rock. John C. Fremont wrote in his journal on October 7, 1843, "We came suddenly in sight of the broad green line of the valley of the Riviere Boisee (wooded river), black near the gorge where it debouches into the plains, with high precipices of basalt, between the walls of which it passes, on emerging from the mountains..." James Field wrote in his journal on August 22, 1845, "This river, at the point we first struck it comes out of a range of mountains between walls of perpendicular rocks several hundred feet high." Despite these generous proportions attributed to the Black Cliffs, there was probably nobody climbing them. Limited room in the emigrants' prairie schooners meant that unnecessary items such as pianos, fancy undergarments, and climbing gear

Introduction

had to be left behind in Missouri.

In 1862, gold was discovered in the Boise Basin and the whole Boise region was profoundly changed forever. A small group of prospectors led by Moses Splawn and George W. Grimes entered the Boise Basin after an Indian known as Bannock Louie told them there was gold there. This turned out to be a very good tip and soon a gold rush was on. Mining camps sprang up quickly and one of them, Idaho City, became the largest settlement in the northwest. In 1863, the influx of miners to the Boise Basin, as well as the continuous flow of emigrants along the Oregon Trail, prompted the installation of a military fort in the Boise Valley. Soon an agricultural community sprouted up alongside the fort to answer the need for food and supplies at the Boise Basin camps. This tiny community was named Boise for the river whose banks it paralleled. Boise would continue to thrive after the gold rush ended, but the Boise Basin settlements surrendered to ghostly emptiness and tumbleweeds. As far as climbing is concerned, the only rock the early Boiseans were interested in was gold and the nuggets held little potential for cragging.

CLIMBING HISTORY

It is very difficult to say when people began to climb in the Boise area. Obviously, the area's cliffs and boulders have beckoned to many adventurous spirits throughout the years, possibly even Shoshone youths many centuries ago. The discovery of a small number of pitons at the Black Cliffs during the early 1970s seems to indicate that limited technical rock climbing occurred in the 1960s. It is a certainty that by the end of the 1960s there was a small cadre of local mountaineers honing their skills on Boise area crags. The focal point of their activity was the Table Rock Quarry, which was used as a training ground for "real" climbing in the mountains. Legend has it that one of these local mountaineers skillfully ascended Table Rock boulder problems in his cowboy boots.

By the start of the 1970s, a local ski shop, Greenwood's Ski Haus, was making an effort to promote local climbing by stocking limited mountaineering gear and offering climbing classes at The Table Rock Quarry. These efforts were the brainchild of Greenwood's part owner, Harry Clark, who had previously instructed a "Mountain and Cold Weather Survival course" in the army. For the Greenwood's classes, Harry brought aboard former Yosemite climber (and pioneering Table Rock boulderer), Tom Naylor, to help instruct the minions. The classes proved to be nothing more than a novelty for most students, but one of them, Charlie Crist, would go on to establish many of Boise's classic routes.[1]

---

1. Charlie was also part owner of a gear shop called The Bootworks in the mid '70s.

Introduction

By 1972, while the Table Rock Quarry was well established as a bouldering area, the Black Cliffs were still virtually unexplored. The prevailing thought within the fledgling climbing community was that the

Curtis Olson prepares for the mountains on Goliath (now known as Turtle Rock).

Introduction

Black Cliffs were brittle, unstable and rattlesnake infested. Anxious to climb at the Black Cliffs but unable to find a partner, Charlie Crist ventured out to the canyon by himself and reconnoitered numerous routes via roped aid solos. Despite many days spent on the virgin basalt columns, Charlie didn't see any other climbers for months to come.

Local climbing gained some momentum in the summer of 1972, when the area's first specialized mountaineering shop, Sawtooth Mountaineering, opened its doors for business. The store's owners, Lou and Frank Florence (a father and son team), hailed from back east where they had a history of climbing at established crags such as the Shawangunks. The Florences would do much to promote climbing in the Boise area. Among their offerings were climbing classes, which were taught by Frank and held at the Table Rock Quarry. The new store also brought in some of the era's top climbers for inspiring slideshows. Sawtooth Mountaineering would prove to be "the hub" of Boise area climbing for several years to come.

In the fall of 1972, two young climbers, Mike Weber and Bob Boyles, completed Sawtooth Mountaineering's climbing class. Armed with their new skills and knowledge of rope work they made their first exploratory probe into the still largely unknown basalt columns that Frank Florence had dubbed the Black Cliffs. They chose Car Body Canyon to test the basalt waters and the result was a route they named *The Standard (5.6)*. The rock quality proved to be better than rumored and soon other lines would follow, such as, *The Ramp (5.6)* and *Moby's Dick (5.7)*[2]. Bob remembers focusing their pioneering efforts in Car Body Canyon for about a year before exploring The Tall Cliffs, Mid Cliffs and Short Cliffs where "all of the prominent cracks in that part of the cliff were climbed out within a couple of years". All of these ascents were done strictly "ground up" and according to the "clean climbing" ethics of the time. Ascents were done on lead without any "hangdogging", toprope rehearsal, fixed gear, precleaning or even chalk. If the rope was weighted, the climber would climb back down, pullout his gear and start over from the bottom. Incidentally, Mike and Bob would go on to pioneer many routes throughout Idaho's mountains.

By 1973, a handful of new climbers were appearing on the scene and the Black Cliffs were beginning to blossom as a climbing area. Charlie Crist set the standard for everyone by establishing the area's first testpiece climb, *Barry, Barry (5.8)*. This route, incidentally, was named after a rare neurological disease whose shaking symptoms were displayed before a fall from the climb by Charlie's partner, Barry. Soon

---

2. Moby's Dick was originally rated 5.4.
3. Bloody Crack was originally rated 5.8.
4. The Commitment is now known as White Wash.

other new routes were sprouting up, and it was Charlie who set the pace with testpiece climbs, such as, *Bloody Crack (5.9)*[3] and *The Commitment (5.9)*[4]. Meanwhile, a talented young climber by the name of Tom

Mike Weber surmounts the roof on **Bloody Crack, aka The Roof (5.9)**.

Introduction

McLeod was emerging from the pack offering testpiece climbs of his own, something he would do consistently for the next two decades. Sometime in 1973 or early 1974, Boise climbers witnessed a couple of inspiring ascents by visiting climbers. It was during a visit for a Sawtooth Mountaineering slideshow, that world famous mountaineer Doug Scott dazzled the locals with his ascent of a line that would subsequently be known as *The Doug Scott Route (5.9+)*. Not only was this line more difficult and continuous than anything yet done in the area but it was also picked at random and done on-sight. Also of note during this timeframe, Charlie Crist recalls a visiting climber nabbing the first ascent of the sustained classic, *Surf's Up (5.9+)*, an ascent which further solidified the 5.9 grade in the Boise area.

Another climber of note who visited Boise on a couple of occasions during the mid 1970s was "Hot" Henry Barber. During Barber's visits to Boise he wowed the locals with his futuristic bouldering skills. Tom McLeod recalls that Barber bouldered most of the way up the perfect arête that now bears his name and then magically reversed the moves to the ground. Legend has it that on another occasion, Barber climbed up *Energy Crisis (5.10a)*, crossed the crux of *Lights Out (5.11a)*, and then down climbed *Power Failure (5.10a)*. Barber also managed to squeeze in a first ascent or two while in Boise.

In 1974, two new climbers arrived on the scene and changed Boise climbing forever. The newcomers were a California climber, Dan McHale, and an east coast climber, Bob Jahn. Both brought unprecedented experience, perspective and talent to local climbing. Before coming to Boise, Dan McHale had played a key role in pioneering the Needles area in California; he was also an accomplished Yosemite big wall climber. Bob Jahn's many accomplishments included the first free ascent of one of the Shawangunks earliest 5.11's, *"Doug's Roof"*. Tom McLeod recalls that they were "both quantum light years beyond anything we'd ever seen".

The stage was now set to blow the lid off of local climbing standards. Dan McHale stepped up to the challenge and stunned the locals by shattering the 5.10 barrier with an on-sight first ascent of the Black Cliffs' coveted prize, *The Spear (5.10c)*. During the same timeframe, Bob Jahn introduced the 5.10 grade at The Table Rock Quarry with the first ascent of the classic crack climb, *Burning Bush (5.10a)*[5]. With the 5.10 doors opening wide, Tom McLeod began to nab many of Boise's classic routes such as *Energy Crisis (5.10a)*, *Power Failure (5.10a)* and

---

5. Burning Bush no longer exists due to modern quarry activity.
6. Throughout most of the 1980s, Curtis was part owner of both a local guide service called Mountain Guides and a gear shop by the name of High Country Sports. An avid alpinist, he has pioneered many routes in Idaho's mountains and elsewhere.

Macabre Roof (5.10b). Meanwhile, an up-and-coming climber by the name of Curtis Olson,[6] was breaking a different kind of barrier. At the tender age of twelve, Curtis was emerging as Boise's youngest pioneering climber ever. With many first ascents to his credit, Curtis would

photo by Bob Jahn, 1980

Tom McLeod runs up **Super Crack (V2)**.

Introduction

be a fixture in Boise climbing for many years to come.

By 1975, Dan McHale introduced the 5.11 grade, along with a bit of controversy, when he toproped an imposing dihedral that would later become known as *Introvert (5.11c)*.[7] Although this route was possibly the first 5.11 roped climb in the state of Idaho, toproping was generally viewed as "poor form" and not accepted by many locals as a legitimate climbing style. Tom McLeod recalls, "McHale was the first person in Boise to really feel free about throwing a toprope on something and trying something really hard." Charlie Crist belayed McHale on the ascent and recalls that "His feet were above his head, he was stemming his body horizontally, and it was like watching a magic trick." McHale would usher in yet another controversial change by making use of chalk, which was at odds with the prevailing "clean climbing" ethics of the day and thought of by some as "aid". Incidentally, Dan McHale went on to start a successful backpack manufacturing company (McHale Packs) in Seattle, Washington.[8]

During the years 1976 through 1978, more classic 5.10 climbs were added to Boise's crags and the 5.12 grade was introduced on toprope. Tom McLeod led the charge with routes, such as the ultra classic, *Copperhead (5.10a)*, and the scare fest, *Thin Line (5.10d)*. Visiting hard man Henry Barber chipped in with an ascent of *The Henry Barber Route (5.10d/5.11a)*, which was arguably the most difficult lead to date. Meanwhile, Bob Jahn's toprope flash ascent of *The Scoop All the Way (5.12a)* was likely the first roped ascent of a 5.12 in the entire region. At that time, 5.12 was a relatively new and controversial grade that was used sparingly and Bob modestly recalls that back then, "We didn't rate things like that, we just called them hard."

It was during this timeframe that new technology was introduced to the sport of rock climbing that would revolutionize the sport. In 1977, Yosemite climber Ray Jardine made the first ascent of what would be the world's hardest route using special camming devices he had created for protection. The new devices were called "friends" and the historic route was *The Phoenix (5.12d/5.13a)* in Yosemite Valley. Suddenly, protecting climbs was infinitely easier to do and harder climbs were being established as a result. By 1979, Tony Yaniro, a climber who would later play a role in Boise climbing, introduced a new degree of difficulty to the world of climbing with the futuristic *Grand Illusion (5.13b/c)*. Times were changing.

Back in Boise, by 1979, a new generation of climbers was emerging. This group would ultimately define Boise climbing as we know it today. First on the scene were two high school kids, Tedd Thompson

---

7. Introvert no longer exists due to modern quarry activity.
8. During his time in Boise, Dan was part owner of a gear shop called The Bootworks.

Introduction

and Todd Montgomery, who impressed the locals with their instant talent. Tom McLeod recalls that, "They did the hardest boulder problems up there (The Quarry) right off the bat." Within a year or so, other young motivated climbers joined the pack. The new pool of talent included

Bob Jahn on the first toprope ascent of **Nuclear Sunset (5.12a/b tr)**, 1980.

Introduction

Trent Smith, Sean Smith and future Yosemite locals Pete Takeda and Cade Lloyd. Tedd Thompson set the pace for the new generation with the first ascent of *The Throb (5.11a)*.[9] This was likely the first lead ascent of a 5.11 in the Boise area.

In 1980, new standards were introduced that would stand for the next several years. Bob Jahn led the way with the first toprope ascent of *Nuclear Sunset (5.12a/b)*, which was undoubtedly the hardest route ever done in the area. On the sharp end of the rope, it was Bob and young phenom, Tedd Thompson, who pushed local standards into the 5.11+ range with ascents of *Hex Breaker (5.11c)* and *Propeller (5.11d)*, respectively. Legend has it that Tedd once made a barefoot ascent of *Propeller* in front of his classmates during a high school kegger.

In 1982, the sport of rock climbing was completely revolutionized by the introduction of climbing shoes with "sticky rubber". The new Boreal Fire's made footwork infinitely easier and opened up a whole new spectrum of climbing possibilities. At The Quarry, new boulder problems with unheard of delicate footwork were established. These included Pete Takeda's *Microman (V3)* and Tom McLeod's *Master's Edge (V2)*. Tom recalls when Pete did *Microman*, "Everybody else was still kind of looking for something to hang onto and Pete had the vision to go up that. Everything else was an arête that you went up or you were looking for something to hang onto." Another noteworthy route that sticky rubber opened up was Tom's delicate toprope problem, *Stem Corner (5.12a)*.

The years 1983 through 1985 were characterized by a series of bold and challenging ascents, which are rarely repeated to this day. Tom McLeod led the way with heady classics, such as *Wimp Roof (5.11c)*, *Cool for Cats (5.11c)* and *Nemesis (5.11c)*. On the day Tom did *Wimp Roof*, he was sharing "ground up" attempts with Tedd Thompson and Pete Takeda and he recalls, "We named it *Wimp Roof* because everybody was chickening out going for it." He recalls about *Nemesis*, "That it was the hardest thing we could find that our gear would fit and so that's what we were going after." Other "space routes" included Tedd Thompson's *Lichen Lunch (5.10c)* and Cade Lloyd's *Rock Hudson (5.11a)*, both of which featured a couple of fixed pitons for protection. This use of fixed gear was a departure from the prior generation's "clean climbing" ethics and would portend of things to come.

In 1985, Tom McLeod established *Wire Brush Haircut (5.11d)*, a route that was a benchmark on several different levels. First of all, it was the most bold and difficult ascent yet done at the Black Cliffs. Second, it was probably the first route in the area that had bolt protec-

---

9. The Throb was done without bolts. It is now considered to be 5.10d because the addition of anchors eliminated the difficult top out moves.

tion, sporting a single 1/4" hand-placed bolt. Third, it was bolted and cleaned on rappel, which was an obvious break from the old "ground up" ethics. For better or worse, the new and controversial practice of "rap bolting" would soon become standard procedure in Boise area climbing.

photo by Rob Hart, c. 1986

Tedd Thompson topropes his intoxicating route, **Vertical Slur (5.12c tr)**.

Introduction

In 1986, Tedd Thompson made a trip to Joshua Tree that would have a profound affect on Boise climbing. While there, Tedd had met an Austrian climber by the name of Michael Stoger, who introduced him to European style "sport climbing" practices and a whole new world of climbing difficulty. When Tedd returned to Boise with Mike in tow, the pair quickly redefined local climbing. Tedd set the pace by establishing the area's first 5.12 lead climb, the ridiculously bold *Boogers on a Lampshade (5.12a)*, which sported two fixed pins and a name lampooning the Joshua Tree classic, *"Figures on a Landscape"*. Mike quickly flashed the longstanding project *Chasin'-a-Snake (5.11d)* and then joined Tedd to establish the area's first fully bolted "sport route", *T.V.O.D. (5.12b)*. This route was not only Boise's hardest lead climb to date but also a complete departure from the old traditional ethics. Mike recalls his role in the introduction of "sport climbing" to Boise, "I know what came from my part—things like rapping down a route, cleaning it, trying it on toprope, putting bolts in and painting the name of the route on the rock, which was common practice in Europe." Mike and Tedd also introduced a new level of difficulty with toperope ascents of *Road Runner (5.12c)* and *Vertical Slur (5.12c)*[10], respectively.

The momentum of the 1986 season continued into an eventful 1987. That spring, the first annual Boise Bouldering Contest was held at the Table Rock Quarry.[11] This event was one of the earliest climbing competitions in the country and it drew some of America's best climbers. One of the competitors, Darius Azin, stayed on in Boise long enough to introduce a whole new degree of difficulty with an ascent of his testpiece climb, *God (5.13b)*. This omnipotent route was probably the first 5.13 in the state and it would reign as Boise's hardest climb for nearly a decade. Darius also teamed up with Tedd Thompson and Mike Stoger as they established other difficult routes, such as the mind altering *Drugs (5.12a/b)*. Darius later wrote an article about his time spent in Boise entitled, "Shelter from the Storm", which appeared in Climbing Magazine.

In 1988, Boise climbers installed an unprecedented number of "sport routes" while talented visitors left behind some difficult testpiece climbs. Tedd Thompson led the charge by installing classic routes such as *Petty Theft (5.12a)* and *Men Who Pause (5.11b)*, which were fully bolted and required no supplemental gear unlike most "sport routes" to date. Other locals joined the fray, such as Matt Fritz, with his challenging sport offerings, *Overlord (5.11d)* and *Another Face in the Crowd (5.11c/*

---

10. Vertical Slur no longer exists due to modern quarry activity.
11. The Boise Bouldering Contest was sponsored by High Country Sports. The event was organized by Curtis Olson and Doug Colwell.
12. Bondi Beach no longer exists due to modern quarry activity.

d). Meanwhile, Tony Yaniro, who was now residing in Sun Valley, rolled into town and nabbed the first ascent of a rarely repeated route, *The Sting (5.12d)*. Another visitor, Australian hard man Steve Bullen, was in Boise long enough to establish an over the top toprope problem with the down under title, *Bondi Beach (5.13a)*.[12]

photo by Rob Hart, 1987

Darius Azin on the first ascent of the supreme route, **God (5.13b)**.

Introduction

By 1989, Boise climbing was experiencing unheard of popularity. Bolt protected climbs and a new climbing wall at Boise State University contributed greatly to the boom. Matt Fritz, Steve Young and Bruce Bedell were the most prolific route developers with classic offerings for the masses, such as *Beta Junkie (5.10c)*, *Weenie Roast (5.10c)* and *Crunchy Frogs (5.9+)*, respectively. The hardest route of the season was the airy testpiece, *Fotzhobel (5.12c)*, which was established by Michael Stoger during his annual Boise visit. Meanwhile, Tedd Thompson and Tony Yaniro were developing routes at Leslie Gulch that were harder than anything ever done in Boise. These routes, however, were created using the dubious practice of manufacturing holds and controversy ensued.

During the years 1990 through 1992, route development hit a modest stride with many new routes developed but no real benchmarks achieved. The most prolific route developers were Matt Fritz, Steve Young and Jeff Landers, all of whom contributed classic sport routes in the 5.10 and 5.11 range. The most challenging route installed during this period was *Road Kill (5.12a/b)*, an ultra-delicate dihedral offered up by the duo of Tom McLeod and Charlie Crist. Meanwhile, Jeff Landers and Tedd Thompson shifted their focus to an unbelievably steep limestone crag near Riggins where they, and fellow Boise climber Mark Edmundson, proceeded to develop many of Idaho's hardest climbs.

During the years 1993 and 1994, local climbing became increasingly more accessible to the public at large. Ongoing climbing classes at Boise State University, under the tutelage of Bob Allen[13] and Tracy Goff, were bringing more and more climbers into the fold. Meantime, it was during the '93 season that the area's first guidebook, "The Black Cliffs Route Finder" by Steve Fransen and Derik Casper made hitherto elusive route information available to the masses. My book, "Boise Climbs", came out the following season and offered up even more beta (Table Rock etc.). Also during the '94 season, route developers Todd Montgomery, Trent Smith and Steve Fransen nearly doubled the number of moderate sport routes in the area. At the upper echelons of the sport, Michael Stoger had moved to Boise and quickly installed some of his trademark bouldering traverses such as, *The Iron Man Traverse (5.12c)* and the classic that bears his name, *Stoger's Traverse (5.13a)*.

The 1995 season saw yet another quantum leap in the number of local sport routes installed. The most prolific route developers were Steve Fransen, Todd Montgomery and yours truly. Steve and Todd set the ambitious pace by establishing a number of new Black Cliffs moderates, while I focused on developing a new alpine sport crag at Mores

---

13. Bob also owned and operated a guide service called Greylock Mountain Co.

Mountain. Meanwhile, Michael Stoger ended a long 5.13 draught in Boise with the area's second lead climb of that grade, *The Sting Var. (5.13a)*. Also of note, Mike freed a couple of longstanding 5.14 projects at Leslie Gulch where "Tony Yaniro had left a few projects unfinished so (Mike) had something to do."

During the years 1996 through 1999, Michael Stoger single-handedly reinvented local climbing standards as route development hit a crescendo with over one hundred new routes established in the Boise area. Mike had been focusing his efforts on the "endurance oriented" routes at Leslie Gulch but as he recalls, "I did all of those things out there, up and down and sideways and it just didn't give me any more challenge, so I looked for more powerful climbs which I found at the cliffs on the shady side". Soon Mike was developing whole new sections of the Black cliffs—adding dozens of challenging routes including ten 5.13's and numerous 5.12's. Mike also introduced the 5.14 grade with his disorienting route, *Drunken Sailor (5.14a)*, which easily dethroned *God (5.13b)* as the area's testpiece route. Meanwhile, other prolific developers, such as Steve Fransen and Jay Aguinaga, contributed oodles of moderate routes for those of us who are mere mortals. Also of note, Chris Parker, Scott Bernstrom and Jeff Smith developed countless boulder problems at the new bouldering hotspot, Swan Falls.

The years 2000 and 2001 were a slow time in Boise with only about a dozen new routes established. Michael Stoger had moved to Germany and as a result local standards and development were lagging far behind previous years. The most "difficult" new route during this drought period was my modest contribution, *Rainbow Warrior (5.12a/b)*. Still, despite the lull, climbing was increasingly more popular and the local crags were buzzing with activity.

In 2002, Boise climbing was reinvigorated by the return of Michael Stoger who started right up where he had left off. Among his contributions were two new 5.13's: a direct variation of *Saturn (5.13a)*, and the visionary gear route, *Robinson Crusoe's Workout Crack (5.13a)*. Mike also established some very difficult boulder problems including the seventy-move endurance fest, *Super Mastermind (5.14a)*, at The Peach Boulder. Meanwhile, a bouldering competition was held at the Table Rock Quarry. This event, The Table Rock Top Out,[14] bore a striking resemblance to the Boise Bouldering Contests of the late 1980's, but with a whole new crop of talent. This talent will undoubtedly write a brand-new chapter in local climbing history.

---

14. The Table Rock Top Out was sponsored by Idaho Mountain Touring and the YMCA. The event was organized by Tracy Wilson.

Introduction

ROUTE NAMES

For the sake of historical accuracy, I have tried to record original route names whenever possible. Unfortunately, the fact that people have climbed in this area for decades makes it difficult to pin down the original name of each and every climb. Obviously some route names have been lost in the mists of time and many routes were simply never named. In some cases, a route was known by different names in different circles of the climbing community. Another complicating factor is that old climbs are often "discovered", bolted and named by newer generations.

RATINGS

The ratings in this book were usually arrived at by consensus of the most active route developers in the area. However, some routes have seen too few ascents or are simply too obscure to have a consensus rating. In many cases, the rating is simply a reflection of the route developer's opinion. You may also note that older climbs tend to be more conservatively rated than newer ones. Ratings are subjective and if you don't agree with one, relax, take a deep breath and get on with your life.

In recent years, the Vermin ratings have become the standard for rating boulder problems. All of the boulder problems in this book have been converted over to this scale. It makes perfect sense for boulder problems to be rated differently than roped climbs. The two are fundamentally different just like sprinting is different from running a marathon. I've included a conversion chart for those of us who are old and unfamiliar with the new system.

Y.D.S	Vermin
5.6-5.8	VB
5.9	V0-
5.10a	V0
5.10b	V0
5.10c	V0+
5.10d	V0+
5.11a	V1
5.11b	V2
5.11c	V2
5.11d	V3

5.12a	V4
5.12b	V5
5.12c	V5
5.12d	V6
5.13a	V7
5.13b	V8
5.13c	V8
5.13d	V9
5.14a	V10
5.14b	V11
5.14c	V12
5.14d	V13

photo by Rob Hart, 1986

Tedd Thompson on his route, **T.V.O.D (5.12b)**, the first fully bolted route in Boise.

ETHICS

Climbing "ethics" in Boise have gone through some radical changes throughout the years. These changes have paralleled the general trends throughout North America. Boise climbers of the 1970s and early 1980s strictly adhered to the prevailing traditional "ground up" practices of that era. In accordance with "clean climbing" ideals, they rarely, if ever, placed bolts or fixed pitons. The next generation of climbers broke with these traditions and soon bolted routes proliferated. The old "ground up" approach was replaced by "rap bolting", which has since been standard practice in the Boise area.

Because routes are established via the ease and convenience of "rap bolting" there is no excuse for subpar quality. This means good clean rock, quality hardware, thoughtful bolt placements, and reasonably safe climbing. Keep in mind that drilling permanently alters the rock so please think long and hard before placing any bolts. If you do choose to place bolts, or any other fixed anchors, they should be camouflaged to minimize the visual impact; magic markers work reasonably well for this.

Existing routes should never be altered in any way. This includes chipping holds, retro-bolting and the removal of fixed gear (unless it needs to be replaced). There has been a disturbing trend recently of new holds appearing on old routes. This is unfair to everyone who aspires to doing these routes for real. If you feel the need to "improve" a route, at the very least, consult with the first ascent party.

Introduction

photo by Sandy Epeldi, 2002

Brian Fedigan checks out his handiwork on the first ascent of **Tool Boys (5.10b)**.

THE CLIMBING SEASON

The climbing season in the Boise area generally begins in March and ends in November. Occasionally there are nice days during the winter but it can get awfully winter like. Summer is hot and you will definitely want to climb on one of the shady walls. The Mores Mountain season is shorter, from late May through October, due to its mountain location.

ENVIRONMENTAL CONCERNS

In recent years there has been a dramatic increase in the amount of climbing activity in the Boise area. Unfortunately, this increase has placed stress on the area's environment and some wear and tear has become evident. It is critically important that we have respect for our climbing environment and that we leave behind as little evidence of our use as possible. If we do not, it is likely that we may be faced with climbing restrictions or closures in the future. It is already an issue at other climbing areas around the country, including our very own Leslie Gulch and the City of Rocks.

This scenario can be averted if we all do obvious things, such as packing out our trash, picking up other people's trash and properly disposing of human waste. Do not drive off established roads and don't leave behind obtrusively visible gear on the rock (colorful slings, shiny bolt hangers, etc.). Use ONLY the main foot trails to approach the climbs. If a multitude of shortcut trails begin to braid the hillsides, it will be a highly visible impact that will certainly focus negative attention on our climbing community. Be cognizant of these things and consider how you can minimize your impact. For more information about low impact climbing refer to the Access Fund ad in the back of this book. Please tread lightly so we can all continue to climb.

WILDLIFE

Considering the fact that a highway and suburbia have encroached upon Boise's climbing areas, there is a surprising amount of wildlife. You might see deer, elk, antelope or any one of a myriad of animals. Bird watchers come to the cliffs in hopes of catching a glimpse of the rosy finch, a small bird with the unique habit of taking shelter in another species' (swallow) nest during its brief migratory visit. You will certainly notice the diverse population of birds of prey. Please give all of these creatures plenty of space. Their survival is difficult enough without the pressures of human or canine contact.

Some of Boise's resident animals warrant caution, especially for climbers with kids or pets. Recently an especially upset badger chased a climber out of the Quarry. Great horned owls have been known to attack climbers and their talons are like razors. Coyotes are common and they can be a hazard for small dogs. At Mores Mountain, cougars and bears should be given plenty of space. At the top of the list for frequent contact with climbers is the rattlesnake. There are enough rattlers on the south side of the Black Cliffs Canyon to keep your nerves rattled. They are not as common in the other areas, but they do occasionally rear their heads.

BIRDS OF PREY

The Black Cliffs Canyon is home to many varieties of birds of prey including the golden eagle, the bald eagle, great horned owls, barn owls and prairie falcons. Many of these majestic birds nest on the canyon walls, sometimes within close proximity to established climbs. Please give active nest sites a wide berth because human presence can be very damaging. The golden eagle, in particular, is of special concern due to its decreasing numbers. Historically one or two pairs of golden eagles have nested in the canyon each year but none were present during the 2002 season.

Every spring climbers are asked to refrain from climbing on certain walls where there are established nest sites. These areas are posted with signs by the Boise Climbers' Alliance in hopes of protecting the raptors and preserving climbers' access to the Black Cliffs. For more information about the Boise Climbers' Alliance and the raptor plan, please refer to the Boise Climbers' Alliance page near the back of this book.

Introduction

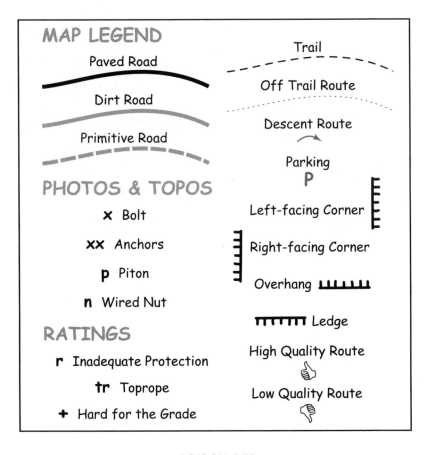

MAP LEGEND

Paved Road

Dirt Road

Primitive Road

Trail

Off Trail Route

Descent Route

Parking
P

PHOTOS & TOPOS

x Bolt

xx Anchors

p Piton

n Wired Nut

Left-facing Corner

Right-facing Corner

Overhang

Ledge

High Quality Route

RATINGS

r Inadequate Protection

tr Toprope

+ Hard for the Grade

Low Quality Route

POISON IVY

Poison Ivy thrives at the Boise climbing areas. Make sure that you know what it looks like so you can avoid getting into it. It tends to grow at the base of shady rock walls, which are coincidentally prime places for climbing. There's a lot of it out there, so be careful.

CAMPING

There are not very many options for camping in the Boise vicinity. There is a commercial campground near the intersection of Gowen Road and Federal Way if you don't mind urban camping at top dollar. There are unofficial campsites in the foothills above Boise but they tend to be popular with homeless folks. Forest Service campgrounds are available at Mores Mountain and along Highway-21 near Idaho City but they are all at least a half-hour from Boise. Last, but certainly not lea$t, there are dozens of motels to choose from if you've got the cash and a willingness to part with it.

photo by Tedd Thompson, 1996

Michael Stoger on his route, **Drunken Sailor (5.14a)**, the hardest route in the area.

The Black Cliffs

Tim Ball reaches for a higher place in **The Temple (5.10a)**.

The Black Cliffs are Boise's most popular place to climb—and for good reason. Pinched between the Boise Mountains and the Snake River Plain, this 2-mile long basalt-walled canyon sports hundreds of routes within 15 minutes of downtown Boise. The vast abundance of climbing includes countless crack climbs and more bolted sport routes than you can shake your stickclip at. Difficulty ranges from 5.4 to 5.14.

There are two distinctly different types of climbing at the Black Cliffs, depending on which side of the river you are on. The north side is dominated by vertical columnar basalt; the south side offers bulging faces that can be quite steep. North side climbing is mostly about negotiating columns—whether it is ascending their faces, stemming between them or jamming the cracks that separate them. South side climbing is usually more physical in nature with steep face climbing being the norm.

For those who have never climbed on Black Cliffs basalt, it is quite different than other kinds of rock. The main quality that makes it unique is its fine-grained composition and resultant non-textured "greasy" feel. Even large accommodating edges can feel surprisingly slick and inse-cure—especially on hot days when the dark basalt literally radiates heat. This quality, combined with the columnar structure of the rock, makes for some unique and challenging climbing. The uninitiated might find themselves humbled by such things as tenuous smears, unortho-dox stems, and a general psychological queasiness. Basalt-acclimated climbers will find all kinds of fun and adventure exploring the endless routes.

The Black Cliffs

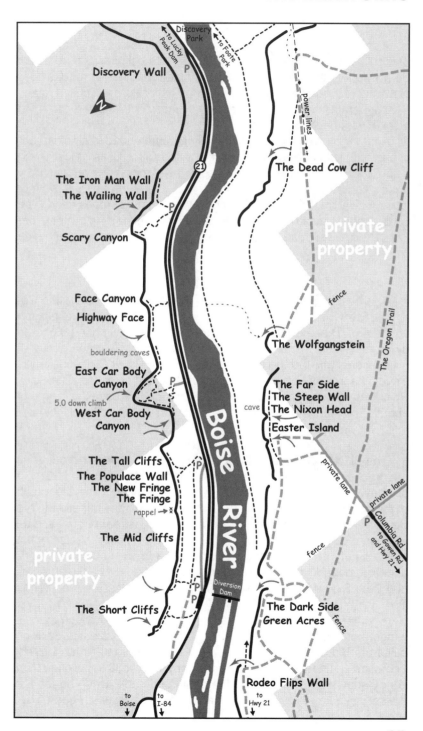

Discovery Park

to Lucky Peak Dam

to Foote Park

P

Discovery Wall

power lines

The Dead Cow Cliff

21

The Iron Man Wall
The Wailing Wall

P

Scary Canyon

private property

fence

The Oregon Trail

Face Canyon

Highway Face

bouldering caves

The Wolfgangstein

East Car Body
Canyon

P

cave

The Far Side
The Steep Wall
The Nixon Head

5.0 down climb

West Car Body
Canyon

Easter Island

Boise River

The Tall Cliffs
The Populace Wall
The New Fringe
The Fringe

P

private lane

private lane

rappel → ✗

P

Columbia Rd
to Gowen Rd
and Hwy 21

The Mid Cliffs

private property

fence

The Short Cliffs

P
P

Diversion Dam

The Dark Side
Green Acres

fence

to Boise

to I-84

to Hwy 21

Rodeo Flips Wall

The Black Cliffs

EQUIPMENT

A standard rack of gear will get you up most traditional routes at the Black Cliffs and ten quick draws will suffice for most bolted sport routes. Be aware that there are a number of "mixed" routes that require gear placements in addition to bolt protection. The fact is, most bolted routes have opportunities for supplemental gear placements and carrying along a set of wired nuts is not a bad idea.

Another piece of gear that is highly recommended is a helmet because rock fall is always a possibility at the Black Cliffs. Most of the established routes have been cleared of loose rock, however, basalt by nature can be a bit flaky and brittle. Also, there can be quite a bit of loose rock at the cliff tops and climbers who set up topropes need to be very careful to avoid knocking any down on unsuspecting climbers below. By the way, watch out for flying beer bottles on the south side crags.

GEOLOGY

The basalt at the Black Cliffs was likely deposited during the Columbia River Basalt Flows, which covered much of Oregon, Washington and Idaho. These extensive flows are thought to have been triggered by a cataclysmic meteorite impact in southeastern Oregon about 17 million years ago. At the time of the flows, the Black Cliffs locale was a river channel that became engulfed by the flooding basalt. The Boise River has subsequently cut its course through this basalt, at a rate of about 1" per century, forming vertical canyon walls ripe for climbing.

HISTORY

The Black Cliffs area is rich in history. In fact, several historic sites are practically within a ropes length of Black Cliffs climbing. The most obvious site is the Diversion Dam, which visually dominates the mouth of the canyon. Completed in 1909, the dam provides irrigation to the Boise Valley via the New York Canal. Just downstream from the dam you might catch a glimpse of the Oregon Trail. A short stretch of the trail is clearly visible descending diagonally from the southern rim rock and disappearing into a subdivision near the bridge. The Green Acres and Dark Side approach actually begins more or less on the Oregon Trail.

Another site worthy of note is the Foote House. Although there is almost nothing left of this structure, it was once a sizeable dwelling built from Black Cliffs basalt. The house was home to Arthur DeWint Foote, an engineer who arrived at the canyon in 1883 to build the New York Canal. Foote worked on the canal until 1892 when he left the project discouraged by ongoing legal and financial issues. Foote's wife,

The Black Cliffs

Mary Hallock Foote was a successful writer who penned their experiences living in "the darkest part of darkest Idaho!", or as we know it, the Black Cliffs. The Foote Mansion site is located near Foote Park on the south side of the canyon.

photo by Rob Hart, 1987

Tedd Thompson summons up mysterious powers on **Hex Breaker (5.11c)**.

The Black Cliffs

HOW TO GET THERE

The Black Cliffs are reached from Boise via Warm Springs Avenue or Hwy-21, depending on your starting point. From the downtown area, Warm Springs Avenue is a straight shot to the Black Cliffs. From the intersection of Broadway Avenue and Warm Springs Avenue, drive about seven miles east on Warm Springs to its intersection with Hwy-21 at the Black Cliffs. From west or south Boise, take I-84 east to the Hwy-21 turnoff. Drive about three and a half miles east on Hwy-21 to reach the mouth of the canyon at the previously mentioned intersection with Warm Springs Avenue. See the Boise Region Map and Black Cliffs Overview Map for details.

THE BLACK CLIFFS NORTH SIDE...

To Reach the **Short Cliffs** and the west end of the **Mid Cliffs**, drive 0.3 mile beyond the intersection of Warm Springs Avenue and Hwy-21 to Diversion Dam. Across from Diversion Dam, is a paved parking area for tourists visiting the dam. On both ends of this parking area, there are dirt pullouts that provide parking for the Short Cliffs and Mid Cliffs areas. To reach the east end of the **Mid Cliffs**, the **Fringe**, the **New Fringe**, **Populace Wall**, and the **Tall Cliffs**, exit the Diversion Dam parking area at its east end onto a dirt road that parallels the highway. Proceed 0.3 mile to a large dirt parking area next to the highway.

Hwy-21 separates into two one-way roads at the Diversion Dam parking area. In order to reach the other north side areas, you must continue 1.8 miles up Hwy-21 to the Sandy Point Beach turnoff below Lucky Peak Dam, and turn around. The **Discovery Wall** is located 0.3 mile back toward Boise. There is a very large dirt pullout. The **Iron Man Wall**, **Wailing Wall**, and **Scary Canyon** are located 0.7 mile back. There is a small dirt parking area. **Face Canyon** and **Highway Face** are located 0.9 mile back with no parking area available. **Car Body Canyon** is located 1.2 miles back. Parking is available just off the highway.

THE BLACK CLIFFS SOUTH SIDE...

To reach the **Dead Cow Cliff**, follow the directions in the Black Cliffs North Side section to the Sandy Point Beach turnoff. From the turnoff, proceed east on highway-21 for 1 mile to the top of Lucky Peak Dam. Turn right on the dam road and proceed 0.7 mile to the signed turnoff to Foote Park. Drive 0.7 mile down the Foote Park road to its end at a gate just past tiny Foote Park. From the gate, walk the trail into the canyon for approximately half a mile to a prominent side canyon. Enter this canyon on an indistinct trail and proceed up the trail to a point where power lines cross overhead. Leave the trail here to follow the power lines to the west and begin counting power line towers for a distance reference. Ascend the steep loose slope to the top of the canyon to gain access to a power line access road. Follow this road to a subtle drainage that drops into the canyon shortly before the 4th power line tower. Leave the road and walk down the drainage, which becomes choked with boulders as you descend below the canyon rim. The Dead Cow Cliff is the wall to your left.

The best approach for the **Wolfgangstein** begins with the same drive as for the Dead Cow Cliff. From the end of the road, hike the trail alongside the reservoir for about a mile into the canyon. You will come to a point were the steep slope between the reservoir and the cliffs is noticeably reduced in grade. Hike up this slope to the small lone crag.

To reach **Easter Island**, the **Nixon Head**, the **Steep Wall**, and the **Far Side**, turn south off of Hwy-21 onto Technology Way. Technology Way is 2.7 miles west of the intersection of Hwy-21 and Warm Springs Avenue and 1 mile east of I-84. After driving 1 mile on Technology Way, it will make a ninety-degree turn and become Columbia Road. Proceed a little over 2 miles on Columbia Road to the end of the pavement. Park here and walk along the gravel continuation of the road. The gravel continuation of Columbia Road is a private lane but the parcel of land directly left of it is public. Please respect the private property. Walk just left of the lane on the public land to avoid trespassing. After a quarter mile or so you will come to an old jeep track that cuts left toward the canyon. Follow this track to an intersection with another track that runs along the canyon rim. Cross the rim track and follow a singletrack trail east along the rim until you reach an obvious descent gully. A BCA sign marks the top of it. Descend the gully and turn left to reach Easter Island or turn right to reach the Nixon Head, the Steep Wall, and the Far Side. The Wolfgangstein approach can also be used.

To reach **Rodeo Flips Wall**, **Green Acres**, and the **Dark Side**, drive 1 mile up Hwy-21 from the intersection of Warm Springs Ave. and Hwy-21 to an unmarked road on the left, opposite E. Lake Forrest. If you are approaching from I-84, this road is located approximately 2.5 miles east on Hwy-21. Turn on this unmarked road and drive a short distance to its end at a very large paved area (future site of an Oregon Trail interpretive center). Park at the far end of the paved area where a gated primitive road begins. Walk toward the canyon on this road as it runs alongside power lines and then fragments into splinter roads. Take the left most route along the canyon rim until it makes a sudden turn to the right and begins to climb. At this point, which is about three quarters of a mile from the start, a singletrack trail heads straight into the canyon to Green Acres and the Dark Side. Rodeo Flips Wall is on the cliff band just below the start of the singletrack trail.

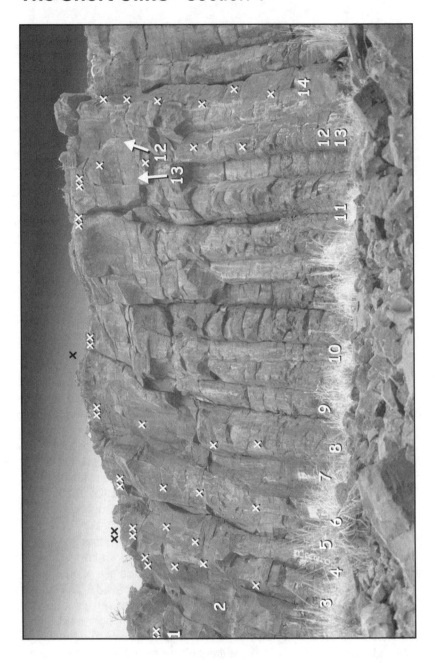

The Short Cliffs

1. **Spiny Trouble 5.10b** (partially pictured) Located on the arête just to the left of *Short Crack*. 4 bolts to chains.

2. **Short Crack 5.8** Climb to the top of the short column and then up the obvious line of weakness. The 2 bolt belay is located over the top and back a ways.

3. **Hilti Dust 5.11b** 3 bolts to chains. Easy moves lead to a dyno.

👍 4. **Desperate Indulgence 5.11a** 2 bolts and supplementary pro to chains. A #0 TCU slots nicely in the horizontal seam below the first bolt.

5. **In Between 5.10b tr** Inside corner to the *Petty Theft* anchors.

👍 6. **Petty Theft 5.12a** 3 bolts to chains. The difficulty increases by a number grade at each bolt.

7. **Rigid Digits 5.10c** Dihedral to anchors. Tricky pro. No bolts.

8. **Jump Chump 5.9** 3 bolts to chains. The jump is just a reach for taller chumps.

9. **Falling Object 5.9+** Climb through the fractured roof. Use the *Safe Sex Subaru* anchors.

10. **Safe Sex Subaru 5.10a** The route name is painted at the base. Thin crack and a bulge with sparse pro to Metolius rap hangers.

👎 11. **No Name 5.10a tr** Dihedral to chains. Rotten rock and dangerously loose blocks lead to a reachy crux at the top.

12. **Win, Lose or Draw 5.10c** 4 bolts to chains. As the name subtly implies, there are 3 different routes on this bolt line. The original sequence moves to the right at the third bolt. The other two sequences are described below.

👍 13. **Win, Lose or Draw Dir. 5.11b/c** This variation goes left at the 3rd bolt and then into the vertical seam. After clipping the 4th bolt, step back to the right. If you desire a more challenging finish, stay to the left of the bolt line for a 5.11d finale.

The Short Cliffs - section 2

👍 **14. Bologna Pony 5.10d** 6 bolts to chains. This line features juggy moves on a steep arete. It is an area classic.

15. Bologna Pony Var. 5.12a Ascend the steep thin face to the right of the upper *Bologna Pony* bolts.

16. The Trimmed Bush 5.10a Crack to the *Bologna Pony* anchors. The bush is long gone but the pumpy hand jams remain.

17. Edge and Stem 5.9 This line is just to the right of *the Trimmed Bush* and merges with it near the top.

👍 **18. Frosted Flake 5.10c** The route name is painted at the base. Crack to Metolius rap hangers. The pro thins a little bit as the difficulty increases.

👍 **19. Neophyte flight 5.9** Crack and a small bulge to chains. Fun climbing with good pro.

20. Overlord 5.11d 3 bolts to Metolius rap hangers. Technical and delicate yet bouldery and powerful.

👍 **21. Basic Training 5.10a** Crack to the *Overlord* anchors. Bring nuts and small TCU's to protect this thin and sustained crack.

22. Lithium Deficiency 5.11a The route name is painted at the base. Crack to chains. Follow the crack line; if you're clipping bolts you've wandered off route to easier moves.

23. Angry Bunnies 5.10c 4 bolts to Chains. Hidden holds and tricky route finding make this climb interesting.

24. Buster Bronco 5.7 The route name is painted at the base. Crack to chains. Big holds and good pro make this climb suitable for all.

25. Aunt Fannie 5.8 This climb merges with *Buster Bronco* near the top and shares its anchors. Originally rated 5.4.

26. Big Fat Crack 5.8+ This route ascends an obvious wide crack that eventually merges with *Buster Bronco* and *Aunt Fannie*.

27. Mystery Route 5.10b 4 bolts to anchors. Balancy smeary fun of an unknown origin.

The Short Cliffs - section 3

28. The Layback 5.9+ Fun climbing with good pro but no anchors.

👍 **29. Another Face in the Crowd 5.11c/d** 4 bolts to chains. Smeary and delicate! You can supplement the bolts with nuts, if desired.

30. Lost Arrow 5.10b The route name is painted at the base. Start as for *Unknown Leon* but stay to the left of the bolt line.

👍 **31. Unknown Leon 5.11a** 6 bolts to chains. Don't use the chimney.

32. Bag of Stems 5.7 r The obvious chimney to chains.

33. Lunch Ledge 5.9 Crack to anchors over the top.

34. Kowallis and Richards Hardware Bin 5.10a tr Dihedral to the *Goodbye Mr. Purple* chains.

35. Goodbye Mr. Purple 5.11c 5 bolts to chains. The intended line does not include using *The Temple* crack. However, an edge at the left end of *The Temple* arch is considered to be on route.

👍 **36. The Temple, aka Rejuvenator 5.10a** Crack to chains.

👍 **37. Copperhead 5.10a** Dihedral and a roof to chains. Excellent!

👍 **38. Hex Breaker 5.11c** This line ascends the face and roof to the right of *Copperhead*. The opening moves are sans pro.

39. The Pink Panther 5.9 Crack to chains. Thin pro at the crux.

👍 **40. Minuteman 5.8** A dihedral and a bulge to Metolius rap hangers.

👍 **41. Swimmin' in Ignorance 5.10a** 3 bolts plus pro to chains.

42. Coupe de Ville 5.8 (not pictured) Located just to the right of *Swimmin' in Ignorance*. Dihedral to chains.

43. First Lead 5.6 (not pictured) This low angle crack system is located 30' to the right of *Coupe de Ville* and just left of *Toddler*. No anchors.

44. Toddler 5.6 (not pictured) Located to the right of *First Lead*. 6 bolts to chains.

1. **Swallow 5.10b tr** Dihedral and a small roof to the *Kip to a Handstand* chains. Please don't damage the nests.

2. **Kip to a Handstand 5.11b** 3 bolts to chains. There are also gear placements below the first bolt, if desired. This route amounts to a boulder problem in the sky. Pull the awkward grunt moves out and over the roof. The first ascent was done sans bolts.

3. **The Puffer 5.9** 5 bolts to chains. Easy moves lead to fun face climbing.

4. **Ajax 5.9** Crack in a dihedral, with 4 bolts to Metolius rappel hangers. This route was traditionally a gear route (sans bolts) and it takes good protection if you would like to climb it in traditional style.

5. **409 5.8** Crack to the *Ajax* anchors. The pro is a bit sparse on this route.

6. **Steep Disorder 5.10c** A thin crack leads to a short steep face with 1 bolt. Pull past the bolt on bouldery moves to Metolius rap hangers. The crack is continuously thin, so bring plenty of small gear.

7. **Man Eater 5.8+ r** Offwidth crack. This route has some unstable rock and the protection is lousy unless you have gear that will fit an 8" crack. There are no anchors.

8. **Lightning Crack 5.8** Ascend the obvious lightning bolt crack. No anchors.

9. **Tidy Up 5.10a** 3 bolts to Metolius rap hangers. There are opportunities to place supplementary gear, if desired.

10. **Loaded Gun 5.7** Crack to the *Tidy Up* anchors. The route name is painted at the base. Good pro, good fun. The offwidth crack and bushy dihedral to the right are old variations.

11. **Squirt Gun 5.8** Crack to chains. The pro is a little bit thin. There is a bolt at the top of this route that allows access to the anchors for setting up a toprope.

The Mid Cliffs - section 2

12. **Loaded Question** **5.8** Crack to the *Squirt Gun* chains. The pro thins a little bit at the crux.

☞ 13. **Little Boots** **5.8** Dihedral to chains. Classic stemming moves.

14. **Jenga** **5.7** Crack to the *Little Boots* anchors. There are some loose blocks on this one.

☞ 15. **Big Head Ed** **5.9** This line has some dangerously loose blocks on it. However, someone started to prep it as a sport route and they might have taken off the blocks. The route does take decent gear but my advice is to avoid it altogether. No anchors.

16. **Fat Ankles** **5.7** 4 bolts to chains. This seems to be a very popular route. Some say it's hard for the grade.

17. **More Than I Can Chew** **5.9** 4 bolts to chains. Whether you chew or not, the final moves will keep you on your toes.

☞ 18. **Rectal Cranial Insertion** **5.9** Crack and small roof to the *Almer Casile* chains. Better wear a helmet for this one!

19. **Almer Casile Memorial Buttress** **5.8** 4 bolts to chains. There is a bolt at the top of this route that allows access to the anchors for setting up a toprope.

20. **Orientationally Confused** **5.8** Crack to the *Almer Casile* chains. Good crack climbing fun.

21. **Wabbit Hunta** **5.8+** Thin seam to chains. Start as for *Orientationally Confused* but step right at the top of the short column. Climb the seam above. The pro is better than it looks.

22. **Sugar Magnolia** **5.7** (not pictured) This route ascends the dihedral to the left of *Lucky Pierre*. Use the *Lucky Pierre* anchors.

☞ 23. **Lucky Pierre** **5.9** (not pictured) Located about 15' to the right of *Wabbit Hunta*. 5 bolts to Metolius rap hangers with chains.

24. **Nash-E-Mun** **5.7** (not pictured) Located on a slab (That's right, a slab!) about 70' to the right of *Lucky Pierre*. 5 bolts to chains. The title of this route is Urdu for "high eagle's nest".

The Mid Cliffs - section 3

25. Bwana the Mighty Metolius Hunter 5.11a (not pictured) Look for an obvious roof located about 50' to the left of *Snake Eyes*. 4 bolts to chains.

26. Snake Eyes 5.8 4 bolts to Metolius rap hangers. There are also opportunities for supplementary gear, if desired. Watch for loose blocks.

27. Stemulus 5.11d 4 bolts to chains. The intended line is done without using the wide crack (which is an old route that goes at about 5.9), or anything to the right of the crack. The moves are delicate and somewhat sustained. There is a bolt over the top of this route allowing access to the anchors for toprope set up.

👍 **28. In Vitro 5.10a** 6 bolts to chains. This is a fun route, however, a lead fall at the crux could be hard on your ankles. Placing a piece of gear at the bulge is not a bad idea.

29. Potato Flake, aka Stereotaxis 5.8 Dihedral and crack to chains. Avoid the dihedral just to the right of this line because it has dangerously loose blocks.

👍 **30. Nut 'n a Sling 5.8** Dihedral to chains. Despite it's name, this route offers fun moves and good pro. Bolts appeared on the route during the 2000 season and subsequently disappeared.

31. Boulder Holder 5.8 Dihedral and crack to the *Nut 'n a Sling* anchors. Stay on the crack line until the difficulties are through, then traverse left to the anchors.

32. Bloody Crack, aka The Roof 5.9 Offwidth crack to Metolius rap hangers. There is a smaller crack, inside the offwidth crack, that takes medium size protection. Bring a large cam for the roof.

33. Mike the Dog 5.10a Climb a crack to a bolt protected bulge, then up to the *Friend of the Devil* anchors.

👍 **34. In Vivo 5.9** 5 bolts to chains. Thin positive moves lead to a bulgy crux at the top.

35. The Wise One 5.8 Offwidth crack with no anchors. Bring along 4" cams or you won't find much pro. Please avoid this line if you see evidence of owl occupation.

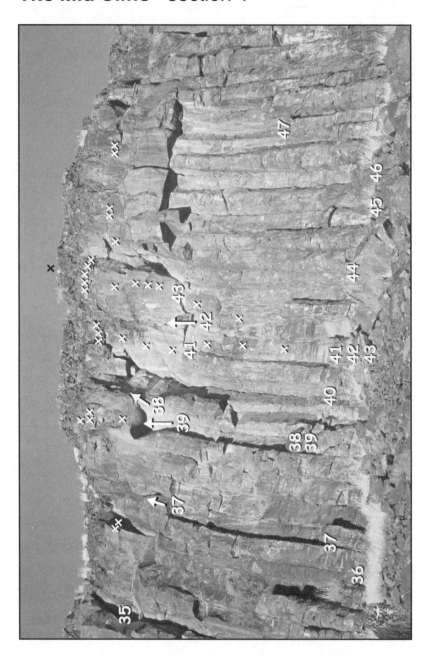

👍 **36. Nikita 5.8** Thin crack to Metolius rap hangers with chains. The pro is better than it looks, so are the holds.

37. Divine Intervention 5.9 A wide jam crack. Climb lightly past the obvious wedged stone near the top. There were 2 belay pitons over the top but they seem to have miraculously vanished.

38. Woolly Footed Vixen 5.10a The route name is painted at the base. Climb the dihedral to the bulge, then follow the crack to the right and around the corner. There is one bolt over the top but you will need gear to set up your belay.

👍 **39. Chicken Wings Var. 5.11c** Climb up *Woolly Footed Vixen* to the bulge, then climb directly over the bulge past 1 bolt to chains.

40. Guano Corner 5.10a Crack to the *Sweat Engine* anchors. There are several loose chunks of rock on this line. Belayers beware!

👍 **41. Sweat Engine 5.10d** 6 bolts to 3 chains. Bring along sticky shoes and some deodorant. There is an alternate finish directly up the prow that increases the fun to about 5.11c, but it's a little contrived.

42. Sweaty Crack 5.10a This short but fun crack is accessed via the lower moves (first 3 bolts) of *Saturn*. Finish at the *Sweat Engine* anchors.

👍 **43. Saturn 5.12c** Clip the first bolt of *Sweat Engine*, then veer to the right and pass 6 more bolts to Metolius rap hangers and a quick clip. Stepping out to the right of the arête to the opposing wall is off route. A 5.13a variation goes up the face to the left of the bolts.

44. The Gully 5.7 Crack to quick clips. A rusty old 1/4" bolt protects the top moves. Climb carefully past the obvious loose block.

👍 **45. The Father 5.8+** Crack and a roof to anchors. Despite a little bit of scaly rock, this is a very enjoyable climb.

46. Oak Bush 5.10a Crack to Metolius rap hangers. The bush growing out of the crack is poison ivy. Aside from some scaly rock and the poison ivy bush, this is an excellent route. Originally rated 5.9.

47. Boot Flake 5.10a Crack and roof to the *Oak Bush* anchors. The crux comes before the roof on delicate moves.

48. Left Route 5.9+ A strenuous fist crack/lieback with no anchors.

49. S Crack 5.9 This short crack is good bouldery fun. No anchors.

👍 **50. Rainbow Warrior 5.12a/b** 6 bolts to Fixe anchors. After clipping the 5th bolt, move left to the arête but don't go around the corner. The anchors are rather difficult to clip.

👍 **51. The Spear 5.10c** The route name is painted at the base. Crack to chains. Excellent jams and lieback moves.

52. Popsicle Stand Var. 5.11c tr Climb *The Spear* to the top of the pillar, then move to the right and pull a boulder problem.

53. Number Nine 5.8 Crack to Fixe anchors. Good pro and fun.

54. Candy Ass 5.10a Climb up to the 2nd bolt of *Mean Chunk of Candy* and then traverse left. Climb past 3 more bolts to Fixe anchors. A direct start in an offwidth crack is an option.

55. Mean Chunk of Candy 5.12a 5 bolts to chains. This route is a pleasant 5.10a face that is capped with a powerful boulder problem.

56. Open Project This is a nasty boulder problem splitting off of #55.

57. The Arrow 5.8 Crack to a 2 piton and 1 bolt belay.

58. Weenie Roast 5.10c 4 bolts and supplementary gear to chains. Bring along small cams and nuts. Don't blow the second clip!

59. Roanne's Way 5.9 Crack and roof to chains. Move to the right at the roof. Moving left is considerably harder with lousy pro.

60. Cotton Mouth 5.8 Climb up the short column and deep dihedral to the same finish as *Roanne's Way.* Beware of loose blocks.

👍 **61. Prominent Crack 5.9** Crack to Fixe anchors.

62. Snow Miser 5.10b (not pictured) Located about 50' to the right of *Prominent Crack.* This route follows a thin seam to a bulge. Finish at Fixe anchors on the prow above the bulge. Thin pro.

Note: Refer to page 112 for climbs 63 through 66.

The Fringe

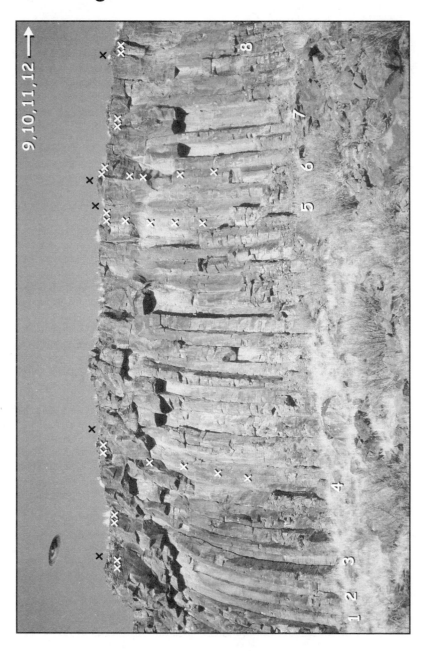

The Fringe

1. **Shit on Flies 5.10d tr** Dihedral and overhanging arête to the *Fill the Bill* chains. Pull lightly on the loose blocks!

2. **Fill the Bill 5.10b tr** Dihedral and roof to chains. The crack to the right is not part of the climb. There is a bolt at the top of the route that allows access to the anchors for setting up a toprope.

👍 3. **Cochise Crack 5.8** Dihedral to Metolius rap hangers with chains.

👍 4. **Poodle Boy 5.10a** 4 bolts to chains. Enjoyable climbing.

5. **Sweat Drenched Flannel 5.10c** 4 bolts to chains. Bouldery.

👍 6. **The Remnant 5.11c** 4 bolts to chains. Great moves! This route is one of the funnest 5.11's at the Black Cliffs but it is also a committing lead that requires a cool head and solid 5.11 skills. Toproping is probably the best way for most people to enjoy this route. There is a bolt over the top for access to the anchors.

👍 7. **The Jim Fall Memorial 5.11b** Dihedral and roof to chains. Are you flexible? A much easier variation (5.9) goes left at the ceiling.

8. **Life Sentence 5.9 tr** This line is 5.9 to the anchors but mantling over the top adds a 5.11 boulder problem. The original sequence went left and was a contrived 5.12. There is a bolt over the top for access to the anchors.

9. **Speed Queen 5.9** (see photo on next page) Located about 10'-15' to the right of *Life Sentence*. Ascend a steep dihedral to a bulgy face with an arête to the left. Climb up and left around the arête to chains. There is a bolt over the top for access to the anchors.

10. **3 Guys and 3 Cracks #1 5.10a** (see photo on next page) Located just to the right of *Speed Queen*. Crack to chains. Ascend the crack that ends to the left of the anchors. This climb shares its anchors with the two climbs described below.

11. **3 Guys and 3 Cracks #2 5.8** (see photo on next page) Start as for *3 Guys #1* but finish in the dihedral directly below the chains.

12. **3 guys and 3 Cracks #3 5.7** (see photo on next page) Ascend the obvious crack to the right of *3 Guys #1 and #2* and then traverse left to the anchors. An old variation goes up the column to the right.

The New Fringe

The New Fringe

👍 **13. Rhus Radicans 5.8+** Dihedral with 1 bolt to chains. Good pro with a bolt protected crux. Watch out for poison ivy.

14. The King With a Crowbar 5.9 4 bolts to chains.

15. Bryan's Route 5.8 6 bolts to chains. The detached block is probably stable but don't jump up and down on it.

16. Sweet Thing 5.9 6 bolts to chains. The bulge crux is a thinker.

17. Bushwhacker 5.7 5 bolts to chains. Big happy holds!

18. Ugly Duckling 5.10a 7 bolts to chains. Short and exceptionally well protected. Don't z-clip!

19. Parking Problem 5.10d tr This toprope route is set up from the *All the Way Home* anchors and a directional bolt.

👍 **20. All the Way Home 5.10a** 5 bolts to chains. A delicate slab finale is the highlight of the climb.

21. Spunky 5.9+ tr This route ascends the face of the detached column to the *Funky* anchors. The crux is the mantle over the visor and onto the top. Watch out for loose rock.

22. Funky 5.9 Dihedral to anchor bolts over the top. Watch out for loose rock, especially near the top.

👎 **23. Feng Shui 5.8** (not pictured) This climb ascends the obvious offwidth crack/chimney to the left of *Stone Tools*. The line takes you up through bushes and loose chunks to the top of a frightening detached column where you mantle onto stacked blocks. The next and final moves pull over a bulge to a slope of loose rocks. No anchors. I would recommend a different route.

👍 **24. Stone Tools 5.10b** (not pictured) Located about 50' to the right of *Funky* and just to the left of the Populace Wall. 5 bolts to a 3 bolt anchor with long chains. Despite a profusion of bolts, you might notice that you're on lead as you grapple above the last bolt.

25. Epic for the Masses 5.7 (not pictured) Located just to the right of *Stone Tools*. 5 bolts to chains. This route was originally a gear route (sans bolts) and it takes good protection.

The Populace Wall

The Populace Wall

1. **School Daze** **5.7** (not pictured) Located about 15' to the left of *Jungle Book*. Crack to chains.

2. **Jungle Book** **5.10a** (partially pictured) Crack to chains. Scamper up the hand crack and finish on the face to the right of the bush.

3. **Mean Adene** **5.10b/c** 6 bolts to the *Jungle Book* anchors. Climb up the face of the column and merge with *Jungle Book* near the top.

4. **Sweet and Sour** **5.8** Dihedral to the *Sweet Adene* chains. The gear is quite thin at the start.

👍 5. **Sweet Adene** **5.8** 6 bolts to chains. Fun bulge finale.

6. **BSU Fantasy** **5.9** 5 bolts to chains. Relatively sustained and fun.

7. **Furst as Sent** **5.8+** **r** The route name is painted at the base. Crack to the *BSU Fantasy* chains. The pro runs out just as the crux moves begin. Watch for loose blocks.

8. **Stems & Jammies** **5.8** The route name is painted at the base. Dihedral to chains. Watch for a loose block at the top.

9. **Populace Offwidth** **5.8** Finish at the *Stems & Jammies* anchors.

👍 10. **White Wash** **5.9** The route name is painted at the base. 6 bolts to chains. Some people like to lead this climb without using the bolts.

11. **Mood Swing** **5.8** Climb the crack until it peters out and then traverse left onto the upper section of *White Wash*. Finish at the *White Wash* anchors.

👍 12. **Perception vs. Reality** **5.10a** 4 bolts to chains. The crux bulge might not be as straight forward as you expect.

13. **My Backyard** **5.8** Crack and a large roof. No anchors. There are a lot of loose rocks around the belay stance at the top.

14. **Little Nest** **5.7** The route name is painted at the base. 4 bolts to chains. There are opportunities for supplementary gear, if desired.

15. **Rotten Nest** **5.7** Crack to the *Little Nest* anchors. This route might have its own anchors in the future.

1. **Full Tilt Boogie 5.10d** 7 bolts to chains. This route features fun steep moves on big holds for its finale.

☝ 2. **Horrible Human History 5.10c** The route name is painted at the base. Crack to a 1 bolt and 1 piton belay. This is an involved lead due to sparse pro and technical moves. Make sure your leading skills are honed.

☝ 3. **Circumciser 5.10a/b** 6 bolts to chains. Don't let the route's name scare you, there are no sharp objects up there. The name is just a parody of other route titles such as: Terminator, Annihilator or *Hara-Kari in a Combine*.

4. **Fly the Friendly Skies 5.10a** The route name is painted at the base. Dihedral and roof with no anchors. The pro fizzles out just before the roof making for some real flight potential. They don't serve cocktails on this flight!

5. **Borrowed Trouble 5.10c tr** Dihedral and bulging face with two bolts over the top. Watch for loose blocks.

6. **In Cahoots 5.10c tr** Dihedral with a wide crack and bulging face above. Use the *Borrowed Trouble* anchors. Watch for loose blocks.

7. **My Stinky Hole 5.10c** "All righty then!" 6 bolts to Metolius rap hangers with an extra bolt above them. The intended line goes directly up the column without using the cracks on either side. Placing a cam above the last bolt will make the final moves much more pleasant.

8. **Hara-Kari In a Combine 5.11b/c** 5 bolts and supplementary gear to Metolius rap hangers. Bring along some cams in the 1" to 1.5" range for the crack between the 3rd and 4th bolts. This route is not as painful as the name would suggest.

☝ 9. **Beta Junkie 5.10c** 6 bolts to chains. The crux sequence at the last bolt is sequential and has been the site of some impressive flights. Make sure you trust your beta dealer.

The Tall Cliffs - section 2

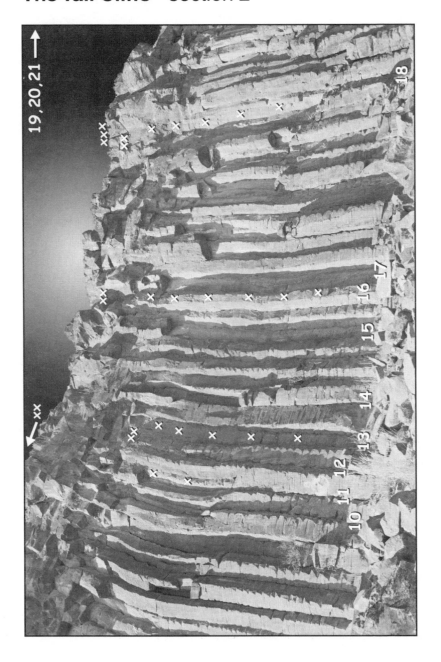

The Tall Cliffs

10. Number Eight Left 5.9 Crack to anchors that are located over the top of the prominent prow. When the crack ends, exit to the right and beware of loose blocks. Bring along a 4" cam.

11. Bosom Buddies 5.10a 2 bolts and supplementary pro to the *Number Eight* anchors. This line was previously a toprope problem that ended at the *Number Eight Left* anchors. The original finish is probably best avoided due to loose blocks.

12. Headlights in the Fog 5.10a tr Climb straight up the serrated face to the *Number Eight* anchors.

13. Number Eight 5.9 5 bolts lead to a Metolius rap hanger and a Fixe anchor. The bolts were recently added to this trad route of yore.

14. Number Eight Var. 5.9 Short column and crack above.

15. Dolly 5.10d tr Climb up the dihedral and through the roof's cleavage. Use the *Thanks for the Mammaries* anchors for the toprope.

👍 **16. Thanks for the Mammaries 5.11a** 6 bolts to chains. Climb straight up the face of the column.

17. Balloon Party 5.11a tr Climb the dihedral to the roof and then finish on *Thanks for the Mammaries*.

👍 **18. Jet Screamin' Hooter Queens 5.11b** 5 bolts to chains. Technical, sustained and fun. Don't blow the 3rd clip!

19. Rosy Palms 5.11c (not pictured) Located on the west facing wall to the right of the Tall Cliffs. Look for a ridiculously short jam crack on the underside of a prominent bulge. This route offers 15' of steep and vicious fist jamming with great positioning. Unfortunately, the crack is accessed via a stack of detached blocks. Be careful! There is also a wedged rock at the top of the crack that is suspect. The climb ends at a single bolt over the top.

20. Muchachas Borrachas 5.9 (not pictured) Located about 40' to the right of *Rosy Palms*. 3 bolts to chains.

21. Joe Pro 5.10a Located immediately to the right of *Muchachas Borrachas*. Crack to the *Muchachas Borrachas* anchors. The pro is a bit thin and there are holds that could possibly come loose.

West Car Body Canyon - section 1

West Car Body Canyon

👍 1. **The Car Body Traverse 5.12a** (not pictured) This 100' traverse is located at the far left end of the West Car Body wall. The intended sequence doesn't use the short column tops for footholds.

2. **The Ramp 5.6** Ascend the obvious line up the right-leaning columns. Watch for loose blocks. No anchors.

3. **The Nose 5.6** Climb up just left of a ceiling and then up the obvious nose feature. No anchors.

4. **Bird Roof 5.10b** Climb through the obvious fractured roof and on to a steep crack. No anchors.

👍 5. **Crunchy Frogs 5.9+** 5 bolts to Metolius rap hangers. There are supplementary gear placements, if desired.

👍 6. **Barry, Barry 5.8** Crack to the *Crunchy Frogs* anchors. Fun steep finale. Good pro at the crux.

7. **Dawn Patrol 5.8** 5 bolts to Metolius rap hangers with chains.

8. **Constant Current 5.8** Crack to Metolius rap hangers.

9. **Watts Up? 5.9 tr** This toprope line ascends the dihedral to the roof and then merges with *Circuit Breaker.*

👍 10. **Circuit Breaker 5.10b** 6 bolts to chains. Climb straight up the face of the column.

11. **High Voltage 5.10b tr** This toprope line ascends the shallow dihedral to the right of *Circuit Breaker* and finishes at the *Circuit Breaker* anchors.

12. **West Wall Won 5.9 r** This micro seam offers very little pro.

13. **Lizard Breath 5.10a** 6 bolts to chains. Good slopey fun.

👍 14. **Ohm's Law 5.9** Crack to chains. Good pro, good fun, great finish.

👍 15. **French Fried 5.10a/b** Clip the first bolt of *Bolts-n-Burger* and then veer left to the other boltline. Climb directly up the column past 4 more bolts without drifting onto *Bolts-n-Burger* or *Ohm's Law.* The route ends at the *Bolts-n-Burger* anchors.

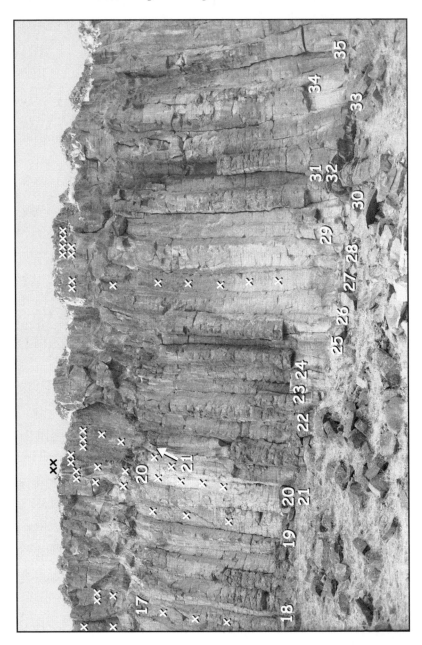

16. **Bolts-n-Burger** **5.8+** 6 bolts to a 2 chain anchor with an extra bolt above. For more of a challenge, climb past the anchors to the top.

17. **Row Your Boat** **5.10a** 4 bolts to chains. Don't blow the 3rd clip!

18. **Generic Crack** **5.8** Head left at the top of the dihedral to the *Row Your Boat* anchors. A 5.10d variation moves to the right, from the top of the dihedral, to a technical thin crack (no anchors).

19. **Excalibur** **5.9** 5 bolts to Metolius rap hangers. This route was traditionally a gear route (sans bolts) and it takes decent protection.

👍 20. **Thursday Knights** **5.10b** 6 bolts to chains. Climbing the arête to the right of the bolt line increases the difficulty to 5.10d.

👍 21. **Dos Pescadores** **5.10c** Start as for *Thursday Knights*, clipping 3 of its bolts, then go right and pass 4 more bolts to a 3 chain anchor.

22. **Arachnophobia** **5.7** Exit to the right at the top. No anchors.

23. **Forgotten Crack** **5.8** Ascend the thin crack on the left side of the platform. Watch for loose blocks! No anchors.

24. **Obvious Crack** **5.8** Ascend the wide crack to choss above.

25. **Shimmey** **5.7** Dihedral and cracks. No anchors.

26. **Mathew's Offwidth** **5.8+ r** The pro is sparse and there are some scary loose blocks. Finish at the *Pabst Smear* anchors.

👍 27. **Pabst Smear** **5.10b** 6 bolts to Metolius rap hangers. This outstanding dihedral used to be a gear route (sans bolts) and the pro was less than inspiring. The original rating was 5.9+.

👍 28. **Stretch Armstrong** **5.11d tr** This sustained toprope route goes up the face without using the cracks on either side of the column. The anchors are over the top and they are easily accessible. A Tyrolean traverse has been done between the top of this route and the East Wall near *Whitehead Crack*. Each end has a 4 bolt anchor.

👍 29. **Velcro Fly** **5.10b** This is a very fun finger crack with good pro.

30. **Wounded Knee** **5.8+ r** Bring tube chocks to lead this offwidth.

31. The Standard 5.6 This was one of the first routes at the cliffs. Chimney up behind the detached column. No anchors.

☝ **32. Steve's Offwidth 5.7** Start at the same place as *The Standard* but then climb the crack to the left of the chimney. No anchors.

33. The Standard Right 5.8 A bouldery start leads to easier climbing. Watch for loose blocks. No anchors.

34. The Standard Direct 5.7 Ascend the crack up the fractured face of the column. Watch for loose blocks. No anchors.

35. The Folly 5.8 Start up the pinched off chimney. No anchors.

36. A Dirt Bag and Lichen It 5.7 A little bit grungy in spots. No anchors.

☝ **37. Road Kill 5.12a/b** 5 bolts to chains. Technical and sustained climbing. Beware of the sharp mono pocket at the crux.

☝ **38. The Doug Scott Route, aka Todd's Crack 5.9+** Crack to Metolius rap hangers. This line is possibly the best jam crack in the area. Begin the climb on easy moves to the left of the small cave or pull the bouldery direct start for more of a challenge. Owls have nested here in the past; if they are present don't do this route.

39. Thin Line 5.10d r The pro for this route is imaginary at best. The smart thing to do is toprope. Use the *Doug Scott Route* anchors.

40. No Dental Records 5.11d 4 bolts and supplementary pro to Metolius rap hangers. These moves are crimpy and delicate! Don't fall at the 3rd clip! Bring small gear for the upper section.

☝ **41. Boogers on a Lampshade 5.12a r** Balancy technical moves lead to the *No Dental Records* anchors. The original pro on this very bold route consisted of two knife blades and a couple of small nut placements. Now it is possible to use the lower *No Dental Records* bolts for leading but a toprope is probably a better idea.

42. Neon Nazi 5.10d r Thin crack and face moves with sparse pro. Toproping this route is the safest option. No anchors.

photo by Rob Hart, 1987

Pokey Amory makes a smooth move on **Kaopectate (5.12c)**.

43. Lancelot 5.7 Crack to the *Flying Circus* anchors. Good pro and fun but watch for loose rock.

44. The Flying Circus 5.8+ Crack to Metolius rap hangers. Very nice!

45. Pictures of Lily 5.11b 5 bolts and an exhilarating runout to chains. Excellent moves. The bad news is that the clip stance at the anchors is reachy with big fall potential.

46. The Throb 5.10d 6 bolts to anchors. This excellent route was traditionally a gear climb (sans bolts) and it finished over the top.

47. Nemesis 5.11c r A thin seam with tiny pro to the *Kaopectate* chains. This superb delicate line is most enjoyable on toprope.

48. Kaopectate 5.12c 4 bolts and supplementary pro to chains. A wide crack leads to a powerful boulder problem on a steep face. When you arrive at the top of the crack you will find out how the route got its name. Stay to the right of the upper bolt line or you will miss the crux.

49. King Arthur 5.10a r Boulder over the roof (bad landing) and climb the crack above. Watch for loose rock. No anchors.

50. No Nombre 5.10d tr Look for the anchors to this toprope climb in the blocky rock at the back of Car Body Canyon. The nature of the rock is unstable and there are many loose holds. Be careful.

51. The Girdle 5.9 A1 In 1979, Curtis Olson, John Rozell, and Mike Weber teamed up to do a roped traverse of Car Body Canyon. They began at *The Nose* and finished near *Moby's Dick*. How's that for an endurance burn?

How did Car Body Canyon get its name? For many years there was an old wrecked car in this "cove". It eventually disappeared but scattered parts remained. As the years passed, a bucket seat found its way to the base of "The Throb" where it would afford comfort to many lazy belayers. The seat eventually vanished and now only tiny fragments remain of the old crashed car.

East Car Body Canyon

1. **Car Body Down Climb 5.0** (not pictured) Located to the left of *Hershey Squirt.* Great Horned Owls have been known to nest here. Please avoid this down climb when they are present.

2. **Hershey Squirt 5.10c** (not pictured) This 25' route is located about 20' to the left of *Terminal Hypocrisy.* 3 bolts to anchors. Blowing the 3rd clip could result in ground fall.

👍 3. **Boys-r-Blue 5.10b** 5 bolts to chains. A very short but fun climb. The intended line goes over the bulge, not around it.

4. **Terminal Hypocrisy 5.10b** 3 bolts to chains. Short but sustained with technical moves.

5. **The Cleaning Lady 5.8** Crack to the *Dirty Luck* chains.

6. **Dirty Luck 5.8** Crack to chains. There is a bolt over the top of this route allowing access to the anchors for toprope set up.

7. **Spasm 5.8** Crack to the *Temporary Insanity* chains. Watch for a loose block near the top.

👍 8. **Temporary Insanity 5.9** Dihedral to chains. A typical start leads to intriguing moves. There is a bolt over the top of this route allowing access to the anchors for toprope set up.

9. **Flammable Idaho 5.9** Crack to the *Temporary Insanity* anchors. Sustained climbing with thin pro. Watch for loose rock.

10. **The Industrial Age 5.8** 4 bolts to chains. Good clean fun.

👍 11. **Whitehead Crack 5.9+** Thin crack to chains. Bring along plenty of small gear. There is a bolt over the top of this route allowing access to the anchors for toprope set up.

12. **The Odyssey 5.9** Crack with a small bulge to the *Rock Hudson* anchors. The pro is a bit sparse.

13. **Rock Hudson 5.11a** 4 bolts to chains. Bring sticky shoes and an attentive belayer. The route demands savvy footwork and a steady clipping hand. A botched clip could result in ground fall if your belayer is asleep at the wheel. The line was originally done with out bolts and was meagerly "protected" with a piton and gear.

👍 **14. Eyeless In Gaza 5.7** Dihedral to anchors. Good pro and fun.

👍 **15. The Scream 5.10b** Thin crack with 1 bolt to chains. The bolt was a later addition and it makes the crux moves much less stressful. Bring plenty of small gear.

👍 **16. Basalt Somersault 5.9+** Dihedral to chains. Great stemming and smearing. Plunging acrobatics are optional.

17. Lichen Lunch 5.10c 4 bolts to chains. The bolts were a later addition to this route; the original protection was 3 pitons. Don't wander over to *Basalt Somersault*.

👎 **18. The Left Grunge Tower 5.7** Crack to the *Jen's Dilemma* anchors. Ultra grungy! Maybe it will clean up with traffic.

👎 **19. The Right Grunge Tower 5.7** Crack to the *Jen's Dilemma* anchors. Super dirty! Maybe it will clean up with traffic.

20. Jen's Dilemma 5.8+ Crack to chains. Fun thin crack moves.

21. Curt's Boot 5.7 Crack to chains. During the epic first ascent, one of Curt's boots got stuck in the crack leaving him barefoot.

22. Up in Smoke 5.8 Dihedral with sparse pro and no anchors.

👍 **23. The Spice of Life 5.10b** 5 bolts to chains. Follow the obvious line to an airy finish. A more direct line avoids the holds on the left arête for a 5.11b finale. The first ascent was done the 5.11b way.

24. Apprehension 5.8 Offwidth crack to the *Macabre* Chains.

25. Defiance 5.10a Crack to the *Macabre* chains. The crux moves are difficult to protect.

👍 **26. Macabre Roof 5.10b** Dihedral and roof to chains. A classic boulder problem in the sky.

👍 **27. Tin Man 5.11b/c** 5 bolts with funky hangers to chains. Climb up the face of the column without using the cracks on either side. You will definitely notice that you're on lead.

28. Big Crack 5.9 Crack to the *Tin Man* anchors. A grovel.

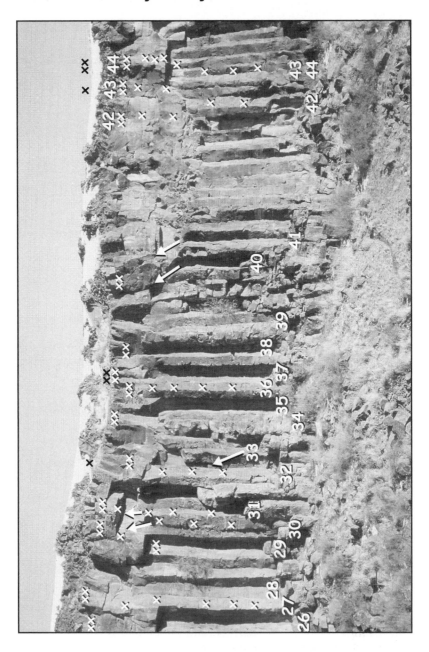

29. **Gargling Vinegar 5.6** Dihedral to anchors under a roof.

30. **Neon Leprechaun 5.10a** 4 bolts to chains. Bringing supplemental gear for the lower moves is not a bad idea. This route used to be sans bolts and the pro was not stellar.

31. **Ambition is Critical 5.10b** 4 bolts to chains. A gear placement before the 1st bolt is an option. Step left to jugs at the roof.

32. **Sperm Whale 5.11b** 3 bolts to chains. What is holding this column up? Relatively sustained moves lead to an exciting climax.

33. **Moby's Dick 5.7** Chimney to a bolt over the top. The pro is a little tricky on this claustrophobic climb. The original rating was 5.4.

34. **Carnaval 5.6** Crack to the *CAS* chains. Watch for loose chunks.

35. **Citizens Against Spiders (CAS), aka Armutoo 5.9** Dihedral to chains. Good clean smeary fun but watch out for spiders.

36. **Holiday in Cambodia 5.10b** 4 bolts to chains. More fun than the name would suggest.

37. **Two Studs 5.8** Dihedral to chains. Good pro, fun moves.

38. **Shake Smear 5.9** Dihedral to chains. An aptly named route.

39. **Stacked 5.6** A thin seam, up a lichen encrusted face, to the *Shake Smear* anchors. Watch for loose blocks.

40. **Whaleback Crack 5.7** Dihedral and left leaning crack to the *Raisin the Titanic* anchors. Do you know how to jam?

41. **Raisin the Titanic 5.10b** Dihedral and left leaning crack to chains. An unfortunate dihedral leads to an exceptional finger crack.

42. **The Pansy 5.10a** 4 bolts to chains. Don't blow the 2nd clip!

43. **Whimper 5.9** Clip the first 3 bolts of *Wimp Roof*, then veer left and pass 2 more bolts en route to chains.

44. **Wimp Roof 5.11c** 7 bolts to chains. Great positioning! This route was a bold test piece climb before the bolts were added.

Highway Face

Highway Face

1. **The Plastic Yuppie Cookie Cutter 5.10a** (not pictured) Located about 30 yards to the left of *Beta Sponge*. Crack to Metolius rap hangers. Climb up a short fractured dihedral to a low angled ramp that is littered with loose rocks (be careful!). Clip the bolt at the top of the ramp to reduce the outward pull on gear you place above. Continue up the obvious steep crack past a loose block to anchors.

2. **Mammon 5.10a** A nice finger crack leads to a mediocre dihedral. Bring along lots of small gear. There are no anchors but the *Beta Sponge* anchors will suffice. Expect some loose rock and grunge.

3. **Riccio's Face 5.10d tr** A tricky start leads to easier climbing. Watch for loose blocks. Use the *Beta Sponge* anchors.

4. **Beta Sponge 5.11a** 6 bolts to quick clips. The 2nd clip is tricky and if botched could result in ground fall. Be careful.

5. **Ren & Stemmy 5.11a** 6 bolts to chains. Are you animated enough to do this ridiculous stem? A runout at the top can be eliminated with a small cam placement.

6. **The Henry Barber Route 5.10d/5.11a** An obvious crack leads to a wild bulge that doesn't take pro. Henry Barber led this route onsight back in the days of yore. There are no anchors.

7. **Soft Parade 5.12a** 5 bolts with funky hangers to chains. Climb up the column without stemming out right into the dihedral. If you are doing the crux moves of *Firefighter,* you are just a bit off route. Avoid this delicate smeary route if it's a hot day.

8. **Firefighter 5.10a** 3 bolts and supplementary gear to Metolius rap anchors. This was a very bold lead before the bolts were added.

9. **Modern Mythology 5.10b** (not pictured) Located 25' to the right of *Firefighter*. 7 bolts to Metolius rap hangers. Be careful on the easy moves to the 2nd bolt because there is ground fall potential.

10. **Unclaimed 5.10d tr** (not pictured) Located just to the right of *Modern Mythology*. A blocky face leads to anchors comprised of 2 bolts with standard hangers. Watch for loose blocks.

11. **The Highway Face Traverse 5.12d** Start 15' left of *Pizza Face* (see next page) and traverse the entire length of the Highway Face.

Face Canyon - section 1

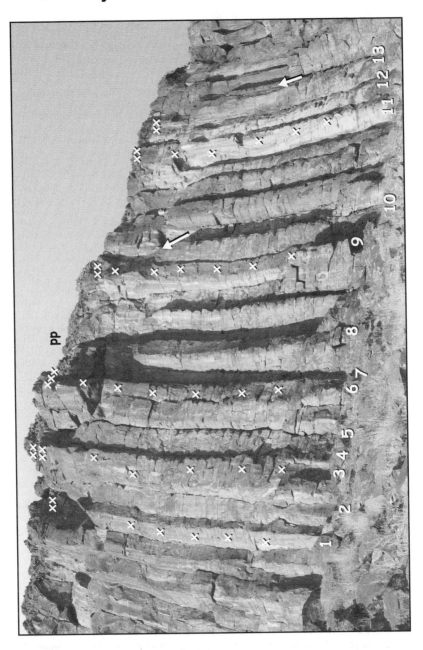

1. **Pizza Face** **5.11b/c** 5 bolts to chains. Stick clip the 1st bolt or protect the opening moves with a nut placement. This technical and sustained route was originally rated 5.10d.

2. **Surf's Up** **5.9+** Dihedral and crack to the *Pizza Face* chains. "Awesome dude!"

3. **Your Face or Mine** **5.11c** 5 bolts to chains. Climb up the face without using the cracks on either side of the column. A bit sporty.

4. **Flotsam** **5.9+** Crack to the *Your Face or Mine* chains. Bring lots of small gear.

5. **Cave Left, aka Family Man** **5.9+** Crack to the *Your Face or Mine* chains. The sloper jugs are surprisingly pumpy. Originally rated 5.8.

6. **Happy Face** **5.11b** 6 bolts to chains. Stay out of the chimney at the top or you will miss the crux moves.

7. **Cave Right** **5.8** Spelunk your way up this crack to the *Happy Face* chains.

8. **Mourning Star** **5.8+** Dihedral to a 2-piton belay over the top (if the pitons are still there). Bring plenty of small gear and be careful on the rotten band of rock at the top.

9. **Steal Your Face** **5.11b** 6 bolts to chains. The intended line finishes on the arete. You will probably notice that you're on lead.

10. **Thunder Face** **5.10a** Climb up the dihedral until it peters out and then head left for the *Steal Your Face* chains. Thin pro.

11. **In Your Face** **5.11a/b** 5 bolts to chains. Some people bring small cams to protect the final moves.

12. **Abandoned Project** **5.10c** **tr** Dihedral to chains. There is a fun 5.11a variation to the left.

13. **Disco Crack** **5.10a** Crack to the *Abandoned Project* anchors. The junky offwidth crack leads to a very nice thin crack. Bring along #0 TCU's.

Face Canyon - section 2

14. **Helios 5.9+** Crack to Metolius rap hangers. This is a short but high quality climb that requires crack skills and good footwork.

15. **Scapula 5.8** Chimney up to the top of the short columns and then climb the obvious cracks above. The *Buttface* anchors can be used.

16. **Buttface 5.10b** 4 bolts to chains. Take along nuts to avoid a run-out to the chains.

17. **Beavis 5.9** Dihedral to the *Buttface* chains. This is a fairly serious lead with thin pro.

18. **Tom Cat 5.10d r** Thin seam to chains. The technical and sustained climbing is very enjoyable on toprope.

19. **Cool for Cats 5.11c r** Thin crack to the *Tom Cat* chains. The sparse pro is supplemented by one piton that is not visible from the ground. This route is very enjoyable on toprope.

20. **Bad Dog 5.10b** 4 bolts and supplementary pro (small cams) to chains. Don't be a bad dog and sneak over to the *Good Dog* crack!

21. **Good Dog 5.9** Crack to the *Bad Dog* chains. Fairly sustained climbing with good protection.

22. **Black Magic 5.9 r** This route ascends the dark water-stained face and dihedral. No anchors.

23. **Loss of Face 5.10a** 5 bolts to chains. This route offers continuous climbing with no obvious crux. You will probably notice that you're on lead as you approach the last bolt.

24. **Energy Crisis 5.10a** This route is one of the best crack climbs at the cliffs. No anchors.

25. **Lights Out 5.11a** 6 bolts to quick clips. A mediocre start with some questionable blocks leads to an outstanding finish. Placing a small cam before the first bolt is a very good idea.

26. **Power Failure 5.10a** A very aptly titled crack climb. The initially thin crack progressively widens and becomes a strenuous offwidth at the top. Bring the biggest gear you have. There are no anchors but the *Lights Out* anchors can be used.

Face Canyon - section 3

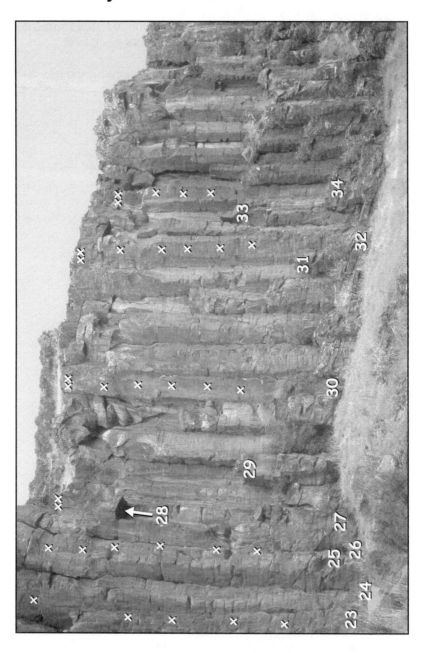

27. **Almond Roof** **5.9** Ascend the dihedral to the roof and then step right. Follow the crack to Metolius rap anchors.

28. **Dying for Dollars** **5.11d** **tr** This boulder problem in the sky is a variation of *Almond Roof*. Climb up the *Almond Roof* dihedral and then grovel directly over the ceiling.

29. **Easy Crack** **5.6** Scramble up behind the short column and then climb up the obvious crack. There are a lot of positive holds and good pro. A delicate traverse affords access to the *Almond Roof* anchors.

30. **Max V** **5.11b** 5 bolts to chains. Great moves at the top! Stay out of the crack to the left or you will miss all the fun.

31. **Saving Face** **5.9+** Crack to the *Dog Face* anchors. This is an excellent finger crack. Bring plenty of small gear.

32. **Dog Face** **5.11a** 5 bolts to Metolius rap hangers. These fun delicate moves probably require opposable thumbs—sorry K-9's.

33. **Liberty Crack** **5.9** Start as for *Cat Face* but step left just below the first *Cat Face* bolt to the big ledge. Climb the obvious crack to the *Cat Face* anchors.

34. **Cat Face** **5.10a** 3 bolts and supplementary pro to Metolius rap hangers. Climb up the dihedral and face to an invigorating mantel at the anchors.

Scary Canyon - section 1

1. **Public Service 5.10b** 7 bolts to widely spaced Metolius rap hangers. Climbing directly up the column will boost the difficulty to 5.11a.

2. **Chronic Load 5.11b** 7 bolts to chains. A quick crux leads to fun 5.10 climbing. Be careful at the second clip.

3. **Onion Boy 5.10c** 8 bolts to chains. A thin boulder problem leads to an enjoyable 5.9 crack and dihedral.

4. **Inbred 5.10b tr** Crack to the *Onion Boy* chains. Flaky rock and lousy pro make this route best enjoyed on toprope.

5. **Simple Physics 5.10a** 6 bolts to chains. Fairly sustained climbing with compelling movement of a non-quantum nature. Be careful at the second clip.

6. **Doctor Hemlock 5.10a** 6 bolts to the *Simple Physics* chains. Climb up the crack past 4 bolts and then merge with the upper portion of *Simple Physics*.

7. **Full Bred 5.10a** 5 bolts to Metolius rap hangers. In past years there has been a Sparrow Hawk nest near this route. Please do not climb here if you see any signs of occupation.

8. **Allison Wonderland 5.10c** 6 bolts to chains. A technical and sustained climb that requires some imagination.

9. **Alcohol Poisoning 5.10a** Crack to the *Allison Wonderland* chains. Good pro and infinitely more fun than drinking too much.

10. **No Pro 5.10a/b r** Dihedral to the *Allison Wonderland* anchors. The pro is sparse to non-existent. Toproping is the smartest plan.

11. **Hot Flash 5.11b** (see photo on next page) This route is a variation of *Men Who Pause*. Begin by bouldering over the small roof at the base of the column. Climb 15'-20' up the column (no bolts) and then start traversing up toward Men Who Pause. Avoid the blocky roofs as you merge with Men Who Pause at its fifth bolt. Continue up Men Who Pause.

12. **Men Who Pause 5.11b** (see photo on next page) 6 bolts to chains. A smeary dihedral leads to a fun overhanging arête and pocketed face. Some say its a bit stout for the grade.

13. **Men Who Pause Var. 5.12a** Start as for *Men Who Pause* but stay to the right of the upper bolts. The upper headwall is steep, pocketed and fun. A small cam placement will make the final moves much less stressful.

👍 14. **Married Man 5.10a** Crack to chains. This prominent dihedral weds excellent sustained climbing with good pro.

👍 15. **Beef Curtain 5.10d** 7 bolts to chains. This route will keep you on your toes with its many devious moves and hair-raising crux.

👍 16. **The Sting 5.12d** 4 bolts and supplementary pro to the *Beef Curtain chains*. Climb up the dihedral and then over the roof via the crack. You will hate this climb if you have thick fingers.

17. **The Sting Var. 5.13a** Climb *The Sting* to the roof. Pull the roof to the left of *The Sting* crack and then crimp past 2 bolts to the *Beef Curtain* anchors. Don't exit left of the roof or you'll miss all the fun.

👍 18. **Flight 1713 5.11c** 4 bolts and Supplementary pro to chains. The layback finale will place you well above the last bolt with a healthy pump. Bon Voyage!

👍 19. **Mind Killer 5.11c** 7 bolts to chains. The big blocky roofs and nauseating exposure can definitely mess with your head. Bring along a stickclip and long quick draws.

20. **Bird Shit Man 5.12a r** This route is a variation of *Mind Killer*. Climb past the first three bolts of *Mind Killer* and then move left toward the biggest roof. Pull through the roof, which offers reasonable gear placements until near the lip. Above the roof, move back right toward *Mind Killer* on dangerously loose and unprotectable terrain. Finish as for *Mind Killer*.

21. **Project** This project has been dormant for several years. Looks like an interesting line.

22. **Short but Sweet 5.11c** (not pictured) Located about 70' to the right of *Mind Killer*. 1 bolt and supplementary pro (small cams) to chains. It's a brief but fun climb on good rock.

23. **Three Amigos 5.12a tr** (not pictured) Located just right of *Short but Sweet*. Grovel over the wild and woolly shin-shredding roof.

The Wailing Wall

The Wailing Wall

1. **Genesis 3:7 5.6** (not pictured) Located about 25' to the left of *Psalm 23*. The route ascends an obvious double crack system on the face of a wide column.

2. **Sixty-Three 5.8** Stem up the dihedral. No anchors.

3. **Psalm 23 Left 5.10a** 3 bolts to chains. Climb up the dihedral to the left of the bolt line.

4. **Psalm 23 Right 5.10c** Clip the same bolts as *Psalm 23 Left* but Follow the bolt line closely.

5. **Psalm 55 5.10a** 3 bolts to chains. Some gentiles prefer placing a nut before clipping the first bolt, some even stick clip.

6. **Wailing Offwidth 5.8** The *Revelations 13:1* anchors can be used.

7. **Revelations 13:1 5.11c tr** This delicate face is a short but enjoyable toprope problem. Access the anchors from *Red Toenails*.

8. **Red Toenails 5.9+** 4 bolts lead to chains that are to the right of the bolt line. Don't bumble that 3rd clip!

9. **Red Toenails Var. 5.8** Climb directly below the *Red Toenails* chains and clip the bolts to your left.

10. **Deuteronomy 23:13 5.8** Crack to the *Red Toenails* chains.

THE IRON MAN WALL

11. **Mental Block 5.9** (not pictured) This 30' route is located approximately 100 yards to the right of *Red Toenails*. The route Starts at a prominent left facing arch and follows a finger crack to Metolius rap hangers. There is a golden eagle nest directly above the route. These birds are very sensitive to human presence and the routes in this area should not be climbed between February and July.

12. **Gravity Bath 5.10a/b** (not pictured) Located about 30' to the right of *Mental Block*. Look for a column with a distinct wavelike feature. 3 bolts to Metolius rap hangers.

13. **The Iron Man Traverse 5.12c** (not pictured) This traverse begins roughly 20' to the left of *Gravity Bath* and ends about 140' to the right, near a painted #5. Don't use the detached blocks.

The Dead Cow Cliff

The Dead Cow Cliff

1. **Gnarly Stump 5.9** Crack to the *How Now Brown Cow* anchors. This jam crack is rarely done and it has become well vegetated. Bring extra 3" cams.

2. **How Now Brown Cow 5.11a** 4 bolts to Metolius rap hangers. The crux move is reachy and will likely frustrate shorter climbers. There have been comments that this route is tricky for the grade.

3. **Black Angus 5.13a** 5 bolts to Metolius rap hangers. Climb out the left side of the roof.

4. **Black Angus with Power 5.13b** This variation of *Black Angus* offers a more difficult finish for those who feel that 5.13a is not hard enough. Start as for *Black Angus* but move to the right at the roof where *Black Angus* goes left. Finish at the *Black Angus* anchors. Mike says, "don't use the overhead upside down foot lock rest or the grade will slightly ease".

5. **Super Cacho 5.13d/5.14a** Climb past 3 bolts on *Mad Cow Disease* and then traverse left past a bolt to the finish of *Black Angus with Power.* "Don't use the overhead upside down foot lock rest or the grade will slightly ease".

6. **Mad Cow Disease 5.13d** 5 bolts to anchors. Do you think you can survive this malady?

7. **Matilda's Mad Cow Disease 5.13b** Climb up *Matilda* to its top bolt and then traverse left, past a bolt, to the finish of *Mad Cow Disease*.

8. **Matilda 5.11c** 4 bolts to funky anchors. This route would be a classic if it was longer than a boulder problem. Great positioning!

The Wolfgangstein

The Wolfgangstein

👍 1. **Bretteljause** **5.10a** Crack to the *Red Bull* anchors. This line will test your crack climbing skills and make you grovel. Good pro.

2. **Hufs** **5.12d** 6 bolts to the *Red Bull* anchors. Climb past 4 bolts and then merge with *Red Bull*. The opening moves are a worthy boulder problem.

👍 3. **Red Bull** **5.12b** 5 bolts to Metolius rap hangers. A funky boulder problem leads to easier climbing above. The crack to the right of the last bolt is not meant to be part of the climb.

4. **Bullworker** **5.12c** 5 bolts to the *Red Bull* anchors. Clip the first bolt of *Red Bull* and then climb to the right passing 3 bolts. Rejoin *Red Bull* near the top. The crux of the climb is the traverse from *Red Bull*, which includes a very dicey clip. A direct start from the obvious large boulder eliminates the crux and makes the climb considerably easier than its rating.

5. **Jump Start** **5.11c** 8 bolts to anchors. This route consists of a series of awkward mantels that begin with a jump start. Enjoy!

The Far Side

The Far Side

1. **El Hedor 5.10a r** Clip the first 3 bolts of *Greetings from Brownie* and then traverse left to a crack. Continue up the crack to the *G.f.B.* anchors. The crux moves are not well protected.

2. **Greetings from Brownie 5.11d** 6 bolts to anchors. This route was named for an unfortunate bovine whose remains are wedged in a chimney above. The climbing is tweaky and balancy.

3. **Offwidth Boulder Problem V1** (not pictured) Located on the backside of a large boulder in the general vicinity of *Greetings from Brownie*. Sit start.

4. **Kaminwurtzen 5.10b** 5 bolts to Metolius rap hangers. This is a fun route if the birds don't get to it first.

5. **Shelf Life 5.10b** Climb to the fourth bolt on *Kaminwurtzen* and then traverse to the right on an obvious shelf feature. Finish at the *Steel Monkey* anchors.

6. **Drunken Sailor 5.14a** Clip the first 5 bolts of *Steel Monkey* and then swing left, passing 2 more bolts, en route to the *Kaminwurtzen* anchors. This is the hardest climb in the Boise area.

7. **Steel Monkey 5.13b/c** 6 bolts to anchors. Explore your simian roots on this impressive arête. If you're looking for steep, this is the route for you.

8. **Wupit 5.12c** Start on the *Steel Monkey* arête, passing 2 of its bolts, then veer right, past 3 more bolts, to Metolius rap hangers.

9. **Steel Monkey/Wupit Combination 5.13a** This route follows *Wupit* to its last bolt (at the roof) and then moves left to finish on *Steel Monkey*.

10. **Bonsai 5.10c** 2 bolts and 1 fixed nut to anchors. Feel free to replace the nut with a bolt.

11. **Chef Party 5.12d** 7 bolts to anchors. Clip the first 2 bolts of *Bonsai* and then begin a long traverse to the right. Cross *Fat Man's Misery* en route to the *Sooner or Later* anchors.

12. **Fat Man's Misery 5.11c** 3 bolts to the *Bonsai* anchors. Tall people usually hate this short route.

The Farside

Michael Stoger strolls up his route, **Red Sonja (5.11c)**.

13. Sooner or Later 5.12c 4 bolts to anchors. Short and straight to the point.

14. Sugar Baby 5.11a 8 bolts to Metolius rap hangers. A tricky start leads to easier climbing. This is a long route and it requires a 60-meter rope.

15. Sugar Daddy 511b tr This line is an alternative toprope start to *Sugar Baby*. Start just to the right of *Sugar Baby*.

THE STEEP WALL

👍 **1. Conan 5.11b** Crack to the *Red Sonja* anchors. Start as for *Red Sonja,* but then move left into the crack. This climb is surprisingly steep and powerful and demands some crack climbing skills. The start of the climb is reached via an unfortunate scramble up vertical dirt and loose boulders.

2. Red Sonja 5.11c 5 bolts to anchors. This route gets a bit confusing after clipping the last bolt. The preferred sequence steps briefly around the corner to the right and then traverses back onto the steep face, where the bolt is, for a direct finish. Finishing way out to the right of the anchors is easier but very grungy and obviously off route. A purely direct finish is solid 5.12. Place a TCU above the last bolt if big air bothers you. Keep an eye out for loose flakes.

3. French Whore 5.10c 5 bolts to Metolius rap hangers. Climb past the first bolt of *Red Sonja* and then take the bolt line to the right.

The Steep Wall

The Nixon Head

The Nixon Head

1. **Resignation 5.11a** Bolts and supplementary pro to anchors. This route was intended to be a fully bolted sport route but the bolting job was never completed. At the time of this writing, there were 7 bolts in place. Another bolt on the crux slab would be a welcome addition. I suspect this route will be completed eventually, but who knows. The route does take gear (with the exception of the slab) and the first ascent was done sans bolts. The climb requires a 60-meter rope.

2. **Ehrlichman 5.12c** 12 bolts to Metolius rap hangers. Four other routes, that are described below, branch off of this main line. A 60-meter rope is needed.

3. **Watergate 5.12c** 9 bolts to quick clips. Start as for *Ehrlichman* but then veer left after the second bolt. The first ascent was done via the most direct line (5.13a).

4. **Deep Throat 5.12c** 11 bolts to the *Ehrlichman* anchors. Climb *Ehrlichman* to its 6th bolt and then veer left. Climb past 4 more bolts and then re-merge with *Ehrlichman* near the top. This route requires a 60-meter rope.

5. **Reducer 5.11c** 12 bolts to the *Ehrlichman* anchors. Start as for *Ehrlichman*, passing 4 of its bolts, and then move right. Climb past 5 more bolts before rejoining *Ehrlichman* for its final moves. A 60-meter rope is needed to do this climb.

6. **The Specialist 5.11b** 13 bolts to the *Ehrlichman* anchors. This route is a variation of *Reducer*. Climb *Reducer* to its 7th bolt and then swagger to the right toward a steep wide crack. Wedge and grunt past 3 bolts before rejoicing on the upper portion of *Ehrlichman* (3 more bolts). Finish at the *Ehrlichman* anchors. A 60-meter rope is needed.

7. **Oliver 5.9** 4 bolts and supplementary pro to anchors. Bring small to medium size cams.

note: The three 5.12's have been climbed starting from the back of the cave. This is an option if you're looking for a bigger challenge.

Easter Island

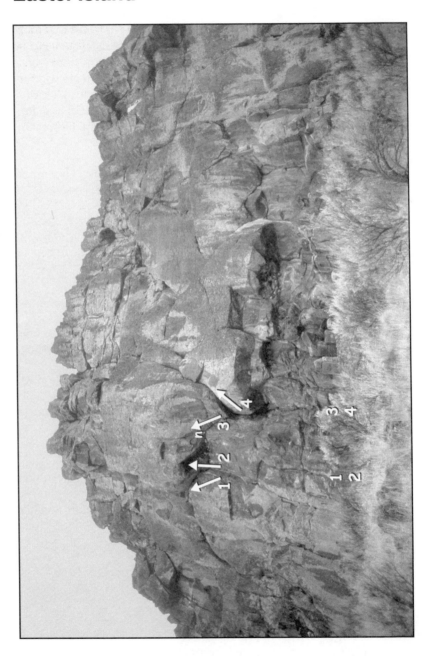

Easter Island

1. **Hotu Matua's Line 5.9** This line is a long and enjoyable trad route that takes good pro. Climb up the face to the bulge and then traverse out left to the obvious corner crack. Follow the crack to the top, where there were no anchors at the time of this writing. Hotu Matua was the discoverer and first chief of Easter Island.

2. **Kon-Tiki 5.12b tr** Start as for *Hotu Matua's Line* but then step right at the bulge. Pull up and over the bulge and then join the upper portion of *Robinson Crusoe's Workout Crack*.

3. **Robinson Crusoe's Workout Crack 5.13a r** This line follows the thin crack that leads through the most overhanging part of the bulge. A 5.10 crack leads to a ten move 5.13a section and then back to fun 5.10 climbing. Mike says that he might install a bolt at the crux "since the lead is a bit committing at this point." There are no anchors at the top but this might change.

4. **The Seven Moai 5.10d** Start as for *Robinson Crusoe's Workout Crack* and then cut out right. Follow an undercling traverse into a hand crack above. Mike says it "is one of the funnest crack climbs at the cliffs." There are no anchors at the top but this might change.

The Dark Side - section 1

The Dark Side

1. **Tippy Toe 5.11a tr** Ascend the lichen encrusted face. A toprope can be set up from the *T.V.O.D.* anchors.

2. **Hobnob 5.10d tr** Ascend the lichen encrusted dihedral. A toprope can be set up from the *T.V.O.D.* anchors.

3. **Floating on Gravel 5.10d** This route ascends the wide crack to the left of *T.V.O.D.* It is somewhat scaly and dirty. However, the exit roof moves are interesting and worth checking out. Bring big cams.

4. **T.V.O.D. 5.12b** The route name is painted at the base. Clip the first 2 bolts of *Chasin'-a-Snake* and then move up and left passing 5 more bolts to chains. Technical and sustained climbing. The 4th bolt is a rusted 1/4" that needs to be replaced.

5. **Chasin'-a-Snake 5.11d** The route name is painted at the base. 6 bolts to chains. Thin and sustained climbing.

6. **The Virgin 5.11b** 6 bolts to chains. Thin face moves and finger locks lead to a steep finger crack finale. Finish on the left-leaning crack; the crack to the right is the top of *Promiscuity Crack*. Finishing to the right makes *The Virgin* easier (5.10c). This route was traditionally a gear route (sans bolts) and it takes decent protection if you want to climb it in traditional style. Keep an eye out for the resident bat.

7. **Promiscuity Crack 5.10b** 2 bolts, plus the top 4 bolts of *The Virgin*, to *The Virgin* chains. The highest *Virgin* bolt might be difficult to clip but it is easily substituted with a TCU placement. Stay to the right of the bolt line. This route was traditionally a gear route (sans bolts) and it takes decent protection if you want to climb it in traditional style.

8. **Drugs 5.12a/b** 8 bolts to chains. This climb will alter your consciousness with its many changes of character. The route features a crack, a bulge, thin face moves, a slab and a running dyno.

9. **Good Friday 5.10a** 4 bolts to Metolius rap hangers. Some people place a small cam above the last bolt.

10. **Safety Dance 5.10b** 4 bolts to Metolius rap hangers. This route was traditionally a gear route (sans bolts) and it takes good protection if you want to climb it in traditional style.

11. **D.O.A. 5.10a** Crack to the *Safety Dance* anchors. This is a traditional crack climb offering finger jams and laybacks.

👍 12. **Wire Brush Haircut 5.12a** 6 bolts to Metolius rap hangers. There are two ways to do this route. The intended line stays left at the fourth bolt for a tweaky crux sequence. The difficulty of this line has increased from 5.11d to 5.12a because a hold has broken off. An easier sequence (5.11b) goes to the right of the fourth bolt on big holds and long reaches.

13. **Fotzhobel 5.12c r** Climb past 1 bolt and then merge with *Wire Brush Haircut.* Ascend past 4 *Wire Brush Haircut* bolts and then veer left, passing 2 more bolts, to chains. It's a long way to the first bolt.

14. **Vapor Lock 5.12a** 6 bolts to Metolius rap hangers. This route is a boulder problem stacked on top of a technical 5.11 climb. Climb past 5 bolts to an accommodating ledge and rest up for the weird boulder problem finale.

👍 15. **Physical Graffiti 5.11a/b** 6 bolts to the *God* chains. Start as for *God* but turn left after the third bolt. Grapple for a very accommodating pocket over the bulge and hoist yourself over.

16. **God 5.13b** 6 bolts (2 of the bolts are side by side) to chains. Turn right at the third bolt. This climb is a very difficult boulder problem in the sky that has thwarted the efforts of many worthy climbers. As far as I know, there have only been three successful attempts. The second ascentionist fell so many times at the crux, during repeated attempts, that he felt the need to place a new bolt.

👎 17. **Melanie 5.9** Crack and chimney. Avoid it if you're not thrilled by a guano-choked chimney!

18. **Project** (not pictured) Located 15' to the right of *God.* 1 anchor.

👍 19. **Groveler 5.11d** (not pictured) Look for a smooth tan face and a small roof approximately 30' to the right of *God.* 6 bolts to chains. Technical and sustained climbing.

Green Acres

Green Acres

👍 **1. Order from Anarchy 5.11b** (not pictured) Located about 50' to the left of *Fairway to Heaven*. This route ascends a crack, through a bulge, to a face above. A single bolt protects the upper face.

👍 **2. The Garden 5.10c** (not pictured) Located 15' to the left of *Fairway to Heaven*. Crack to Metolius rap hangers. Jammin' fun!

👍 **3. Fairway to Heaven 5.10b** 5 bolts to anchors. This slightly overhanging climb offers fun moves on big happy holds. Start on the left side of the pillar for the most interesting sequence.

4. Piss and Vinegar 5.9 A wide crack and dihedral to chains. Bring 4" cams. The pro is a bit sparse for the final moves to the anchors.

5. G W Loves Peanut Butter 5.9 Crack to the *Pigeon Holer* rap hangers. Is that pronounced Gee Dubya? Expect hand "jams" and other crack climbing fare.

👍 **6. Pigeon Holer 5.10a** Crack with 1 bolt to Metolius rap hangers. This route begins in a finger crack that progressively widens until you find yourself pigeon holed within it.

7. Free Sample 5.9 Dihedral to the *Pigeon Holer* anchors. Ascend the dihedral and then traverse up and left to the *Pigeon Holer* bolt. Finish as for *Pigeon Holer*. Watch for loose rock.

8. Urge to Purge 5.9 Ascend the *Free Sample* dihedral and then traverse up and right to the *Feelin' Green* bolt. From the bolt, traverse to the right and finish as for *Irreconcilable Differences*.

9. Feelin' Green 5.9 Small pro and 1 bolt to the *Irreconcilable Differences* Anchors. The key holds were cleaned and rendered usable despite the blanket of lichens that covers the route.

👍 **10. Irreconcilable Differences 5.10a** Crack to Metolius rap hangers. This is an excellent crack climb with great pro.

11. Salad Shooter 5.11a (not pictured) Located about 80' to the right of *Irreconcilable Differences* on a green lichen-coated face. 4 bolts and medium size cams to Fixe anchors. After clipping the 3rd bolt, ascend the arête to the right. After clipping the 4th bolt, traverse left to the anchors on sidepulls and underclings.

Additional Black Cliffs Climbing

GREEN ACRES - CONTINUED

12.Salad Shooter Dir. 5.11d (not pictured) This variation of *Salad Shooter* goes left at the third bolt and then straight up the face to the anchors. The obviously contrived sequence does not include the grungy wall to the left or wedged blocks. The fourth bolt is obviously off line but a small cam placement can be used in its place.

13.Green Eggs and Ham 5.11a (not pictured) Located nearly 100 yards to the right of *Salad Shooter*. 4 bolts, on an unusually wide face, to beefy chain anchors. This interesting but sneaky sequence will keep you on your toes.

THE MID CLIFFS - CONTINUED

63.Loose Tooth 5.7 (not pictured) Located about 20' to the right of (or six cracks over from) *Snow Miser*. Looking from below *The Spear,* you can easily see the route's canine tooth pointing skyward. The route ascends the crack between the poison ivy bush and the prominent column. There are no anchors.

64.Raptor's Revenge 5.7 (not pictured) Located just to the left of *Heat Miser*. Crack to the *Heat Miser* anchors.

65.Heat Miser 5.7 (not pictured) Located about 15' to the right of *Loose Tooth* on low angle columns. 5 bolts to chains.

66.Burgermeister Meisterberger 5.7 (not pictured) Thin crack just to the right of *Heat Miser.* The pro is a bit thin.

photo by Bob Boyles, 1979

Curtis Olson climbs beyond the precarious canine on *Loose Tooth (5.7)*.

Additional Black Cliffs Climbing

DISCOVERY WALL AREA

1. **Chunky Monkey 5.11b/c** Located on the overhanging wall above Discovery State Park. 11 bolts to chains. This steep jug haul is a lot of fun but watch out for loose holds. Approach *Chunky Monkey* from the west end of the huge road cut located across the highway from Discovery Park. Hike up to the left of the loose talus that is below the climb. There are project anchors to the left of the route.

2. **Fishhead Buttplug 5.10b** Located directly above the Sandy Point Beach turnoff, above a large talus slope. 6 bolts to quick clips. This short and isolated route takes longer to approach than to climb. Some of the holds are loose.

RODEO FLIPS WALL

1. **Rodeo Flips 5.10a** Located above a basalt ledge on the upriver end of the wall that shares its name (see the Black Cliffs overview map and navigation section). 7 bolts to Metolius rap hangers.

2. **Misty Flip 5.10a tr** This route is located immediately to the left of *Rodeo Flips* and has its own Metolius rap hangers. Watch out for a loose block, which needs to be removed.

BOULDERING SPOTS

In addition to the long boulder traverses at Car Body Canyon, Highway Face and Iron Man Wall, there are a few small bouldering sites that offer shorter power-oriented bouldering. One such spot is a small cliff band that is located near the Short Cliffs. To approach this site hike up the Short Cliffs descent route and then veer left to go over a small rise. There are also some bouldering caves at the Nixon Head, east of the Iron Man Wall and between Car Body Canyon and Highway Face.

1. **Fire in the Hole V4** This highball boulder problem is located between Car Body Canyon and Highway Face. Look for a small cave about 100' to the left of the main bouldering cave (see the Black Cliffs overview map on page 35). Sit start at the back of the small cave and climb out the ceiling. Continue on, above the cave, for another 20' to a ledge. A toprope would be smart.

2. **Smelly Dark Hole 5.13a** Located in the big cave to the east of the *Iron Man Traverse*. This is the steepest climb in Boise. Sit start half way into the cave at a marked undercling near a pointed rock in the ground. Climb the horizontal roof towards daylight. The climb finishes on the left outside wall of the cave after 20 moves.

Table Rock

Michael Stoger rounds up the dogies on his route, **Beef Man (5.12d)**.

Table Rock is Boise's primary bouldering site. Located within fifteen minutes of downtown, this sandstone mesa is a convenient playground for local climbers. Boulder problems ranging from entry level to ego annihilator are scattered throughout the area. There are also challenging toprope problems as well as a small number of lead climbs.

The nature of Table Rock climbing varies depending on the specific area one chooses to climb. In most areas you will find that the rock has been quarried into smooth walls; at other sites the rock is in its natural state. The quarried sections typically offer footsy technical routes; the natural rock tends toward steep and well-featured climbing. The rock quality ranges from loose sand at the Cave Face to bulletproof stone at the Fortress.

GEOLOGY

Table Rock stands out prominently on the Boise Front with its unique geology in sharp contrast to the surrounding landscape. While climbing at Table Rock, one might see this geology up close in the form of embedded petrified wood and fossil imprints in the rock. These features offer a glimpse back millions of years to a time when the Table Rock sandstone originated as valley fill stream and lake deposits. These deposited sands gelled into stone that was harder than the surrounding soils. The surrounding soils then eroded away leaving the sandstone exposed. Eons of erosion caused the soft soils to recede until the

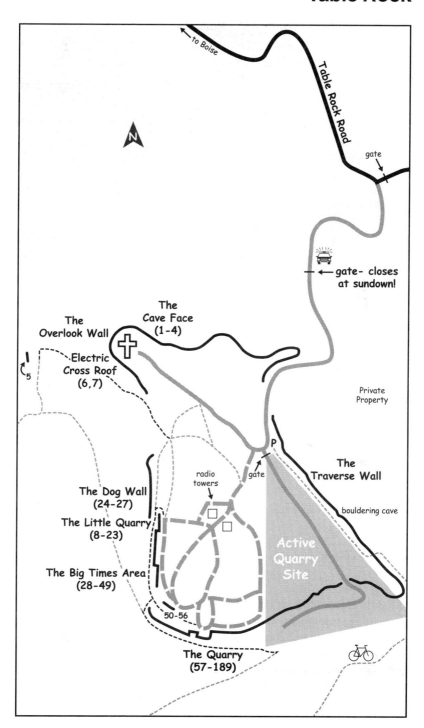

to Boise

Table Rock Road

gate

N

gate- closes at sundown!

The Cave Face (1-4)

The Overlook Wall

Electric Cross Roof (6,7)

5

Private Property

P

The Traverse Wall

bouldering cave

radio towers

gate

The Dog Wall (24-27)

The Little Quarry (8-23)

The Big Times Area (28-49)

Active Quarry Site

50-56

The Quarry (57-189)

Table Rock

valley fill sandstone was transformed into hilltop sandstone. Table Rock was born. Boise Front slip faults then caused sections of Table Rock to slide slowly into the valley. These faults are still active and they are clearly visible from Table Rock as benches extending into the valley below.

HISTORY

For centuries, Table Rock has been an important resource to the people of the Boise region. Local Indians referred to it as "ala-kush-pa" which roughly translates to "the place to build fires at certain times". This reverent use of Table Rock was replaced by a more utilitarian approach in 1863 when the US military began to quarry the site for the construction of Fort Boise. The quarry stone became an ever increasingly valuable resource as the new city of Boise sprouted up. By the early 1870s the sandstone was being quarried by Idaho State Penitentiary inmates who were sentenced to hard labor. These stripe-clad men provided the stone for many of Boise's prominent structures such as the state capital rotunda. Ironically, the fruits of their labor produced the penitentiary walls that imprisoned them.

The Table Rock Quarry was eventually abandoned and enjoyed many years of subsequent dormancy. During this time Table Rock was an invaluable recreational resource enjoyed by hundreds of Boiseans: climbers, hikers and bikers alike. Climbers had recognized the Quarry's potential by the mid 1960s and many of Boise's classic boulder problems were being established. The site was the most active climbing area in the Boise vicinity and home to the annual "Boise Bouldering Contest" from 1987 through 1989. Unfortunately, things took a turn for the worse at the end of the 1980s.

THE ACTIVE QUARRY SITE

During the late 1980s, the climbing community lost approximately half of the Table Rock Quarry site to a commercial quarry venture (see the map on the opposite page). Obviously the active quarry area is closed to the public and should be avoided for your own safety. For example, one climber told me that he was bouldering near the active quarry when a sudden blast showered him with rock and debris. The boundary between the commercial half ot the Quarry and the public half is obvious (see the Table Rock map). The eastern half is the commercial section and it has been blasted into dirt piles. The western section has remained undisturbed since the historic quarry days and it is open to the public. Blasting continues to persist and classic climbs are still broken down into blocks and relocated to landscaped lawns in the valley. May they rest in pieces!

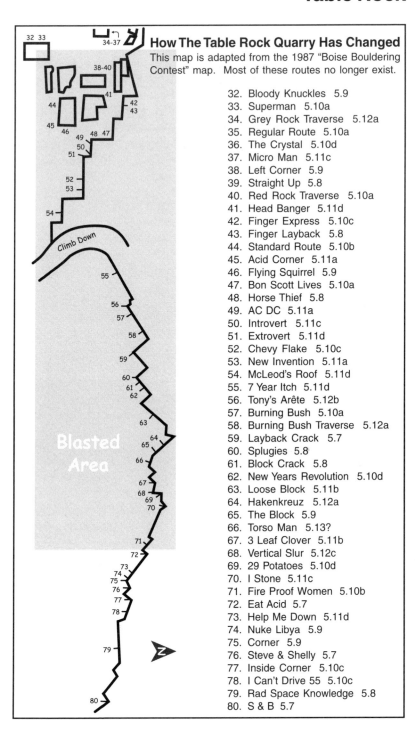

How The Table Rock Quarry Has Changed

This map is adapted from the 1987 "Boise Bouldering Contest" map. Most of these routes no longer exist.

32. Bloody Knuckles 5.9
33. Superman 5.10a
34. Grey Rock Traverse 5.12a
35. Regular Route 5.10a
36. The Crystal 5.10d
37. Micro Man 5.11c
38. Left Corner 5.9
39. Straight Up 5.8
40. Red Rock Traverse 5.10a
41. Head Banger 5.11d
42. Finger Express 5.10c
43. Finger Layback 5.8
44. Standard Route 5.10b
45. Acid Corner 5.11a
46. Flying Squirrel 5.9
47. Bon Scott Lives 5.10a
48. Horse Thief 5.8
49. AC DC 5.11a
50. Introvert 5.11c
51. Extrovert 5.11d
52. Chevy Flake 5.10c
53. New Invention 5.11a
54. McLeod's Roof 5.11d
55. 7 Year Itch 5.11d
56. Tony's Arête 5.12b
57. Burning Bush 5.10a
58. Burning Bush Traverse 5.12a
59. Layback Crack 5.7
60. Splugies 5.8
61. Block Crack 5.8
62. New Years Revolution 5.10d
63. Loose Block 5.11b
64. Hakenkreuz 5.12a
65. The Block 5.9
66. Torso Man 5.13?
67. 3 Leaf Clover 5.11b
68. Vertical Slur 5.12c
69. 29 Potatoes 5.10d
70. I Stone 5.11c
71. Fire Proof Women 5.10b
72. Eat Acid 5.7
73. Help Me Down 5.11d
74. Nuke Libya 5.9
75. Corner 5.9
76. Steve & Shelly 5.7
77. Inside Corner 5.10c
78. I Can't Drive 55 5.10c
79. Rad Space Knowledge 5.8
80. S & B 5.7

Table Rock

ETHICS

Because Table Rock is an area of historical interest, there is a long-standing tradition of low impact climbing. The impact has been kept to a minimum by establishing toprope problems instead of bolted sport routes and by placing anchor bolts over the tops of climbs where they are not visible from below. This tradition was breached back in the 1980's when a handful of routes were bolted and then subsequently stripped of their bolts. Hopefully local climbers continue to adhere to low impact practices, so that we don't loose access to the area.

EQUIPMENT

Here are some things you might want to bring along:

1. **A brush**- Unfortunately in some areas the rock tends to get coated with dust when rainstorms wash down dirt from above. If a route hasn't been climbed for a while, it will probably need some cleaning. Please don't use a brush with metal bristles because the rock is soft and easily damaged.

2. **Extra long slings**- Many toprope setups at Table Rock require slings that are a minimum of ten feet long. By the way, fence posts are not safe anchors!

3. **A crash pad**- Some Table Rock boulder problems are tall enough to send shockwaves through your whole body if you fall off. Nobody wants an injury-induced sabbatical from climbing and nobody wants a sit start stain on his or her shorts.

AID CLIMBING

Please refrain from aid climbing Table Rock free climbs. Pitons can seriously damage handholds. The sandstone is obviously fragile and a few aid ascents could chisel a 5.11 down to a 5.8. There are established aid routes at the Quarry but they are not detailed in this book.

HOW TO GET THERE

From the intersection of Broadway Ave and Warm Springs Ave, proceed north on Broadway (aka Avenue B) 0.2 mile to Reserve Street. Turn right on Reserve Street and drive about 0.5 mile to Shaw Mountain Road. Follow the curve around right on Shaw Mountain Road and proceed a little more than a mile to its intersection with Table Rock Road. Turn right on Table Rock Road and proceed 2.3 miles to another intersection on the top of Table Rock. From here, move forward past radio towers on a very deeply rutted jeep track for about 0.3 mile to reach The Quarry area. Refer to the Table Rock map (page 115) for specifics.

THE CURFEW GATE

During the 2001 season a gate was installed that is closed nightly at sundown to block access to Table Rock (see the Table Rock map, on page 115, for location of the gate). Be sure to leave the area before this gate is closed or you will have to leave your vehicle overnight and walk home. The apparent idea behind the gate is to keep party kids away from Table Rock. Now the kids park just below the gate and pack an extra beer for the short hike to the top.

photo by Tedd Thompson, 1997

Matt Fritz enjoys some steep bouldering and ice cold beverages.

Table Rock

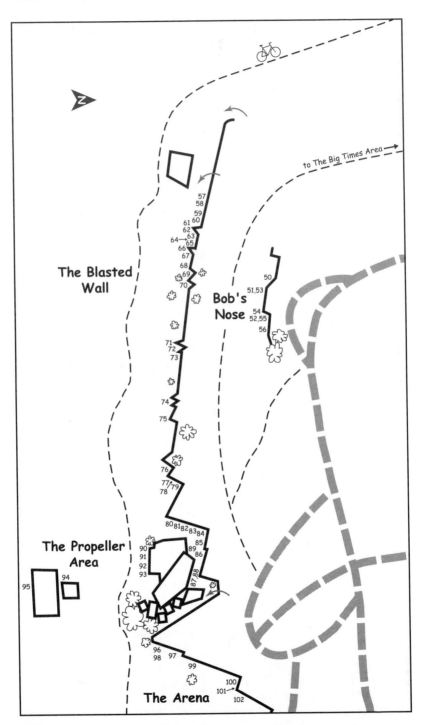

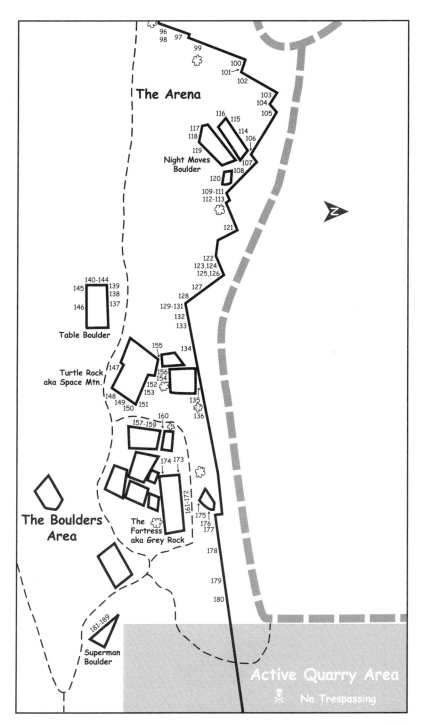

The Arena

96
98 97
99
100
101
102
103
104
105
116
115
117
118
114
106
119
107
108
Night Moves
Boulder
120
109-111
112-113
121
122
123,124
125,126
127
128
129-131
132
133
140-144
145 139
138
137
146
Table Boulder
155
134
147
Turtle Rock
aka Space Mtn.
156
154
152
153
148
149 151
150
135
136
157-159 160
174 173
161-172
The Fortress
aka Grey Rock
175
176
177
178
179
180
181-189
Superman
Boulder

The Boulders
Area

Active Quarry Area
No Trespassing

The Cave Face

THE CAVE FACE

1. **The Mushroom V0** (not pictured) Located about 30' to the left of *Ceiling Crack*. Look for a mushroom shaped feature with a slightly overhanging face to a roof. The final mantel is a bit lofty and lichen encrusted.

2. **Ceiling Crack V3** This thuggish problem is a completely inverted jam crack on the ceiling of the cave. Begin at the point where the two obvious ceiling cracks meet at a perpendicular angle. Jam for about six feet to the cave entrance and then mantel onto the top. Starting at the very back of the cave would be exponentially more difficult. Be sure to tape up your hands!

3. **Big Roof 5.11b tr** Climb straight up from the *Below the Roof Traverse* to the most extended point on the roof. Gain a jug at the lip and start pulling hard for the top. Beware of the sightseers and bottle tossing party animals above.

4. **Below the Roof Traverse V0+** Many variations are possible on this 25' slightly-overhanging endurance traverse. The potpourri of edges, chickenheads and smears might distract you from all of the graffiti and broken glass. Watch out for brittle holds up high.

Electric Cross Area

THE OVERLOOK WALL (not pictured)

The wall that faces Boise, just below the Table Rock cross, has a number of enjoyable cracks, some nearly 30' tall. Unfortunately, there are also a lot of slack-jawed yokels that hang out at the overlook above. You never know when a beer bottle might come hurtling by to join the mass of broken glass below. I would recommend that you avoid this area.

HEADSTONE BOULDERS (not pictured)

5. Headstone Crack V0+ This overhanging finger crack is located down slope from the giant letter B below the Table Rock cross. Look for a small cluster of boulders marked by a switchback in the mountain bike trail. The crack faces Boise and is hard to miss. Start up jugs to finger jams and an interesting exit mantel.

ELECTRIC CROSS ROOF

6. Electric Cross Traverse V1 This route is located about 40' south of the cross. The route traverses the lip of the prominent roof. The climbing is endurance oriented with no distinct crux. Watch out for poison ivy!

7. Electric Cross Direct V0 Climb straight over the top from any one of several points along the *Electric Cross Traverse.* There are several possibilities.

Whipper ⟶

The Little Quarry

THE LITTLE QUARRY

8. **Friction Slab VB** (not pictured) Located just left of *Nova*. Dance up the low-angled face to the right of the obvious ledge.

9. **Nova V0** This fun layback problem will make you feel like a door on a well-oiled hinge.

👍 10. **Super Nova V2** Sit down at the base of *Nova* and start pulling.

11. **Drawing a Blank V4** Start at the obvious crimp to the left of the micro seam and put your flexibility to the test.

👍 12. **Sudden Meltdown V4** Traverse from right to left on a thin balancy face and a pumpy rail.

13. **Santa's Secret VB** Ascend the finger crack and jugs. A sit start makes the problem slightly more interesting.

14. **Junior Achievement VB** Cruise up the lieback crack.

15. **Mortal Cling V3** This risky problem follows the obvious left-facing lieback feature without using the big crack to the left.

16. **Kobe's Forehead V0** Step up to the big rounded jug, smear up, step right and climb into the moss zone.

17. Laid Back VB Located just around the corner from *Kobe's Forehead*. Start at the big slopy ledge and lieback up the crack.

👍 **18. Psycho Braille V1** (not pictured) Look for a face, with a small roof, located about midway between *Mortal Cling* and *The Cutting Edge Traverse*. Pull up and over the roof.

19. Bobby's Traverse V0- (not pictured) The traverse begins at a shallow inside corner about 20' left of the *The Cutting Edge Traverse*. Traverse left for about 55' over a circuitous route until the climbing peters out at a bush. The sequence does not include the top of the wall for handholds.

👍 **20. The Cutting Edge Traverse V2** Traverse from left to right for about 45' and then climb over the top. The difficulty subsides after the first 15'.

21. Pop Tart V0+ Pop to the big rounded edge and then grovel into the lichen above.

22. Zimbo V0 Crimp up on edges following the right-leaning micro seam. Grungy finish.

23. Humdrum VB Step up to an obvious jug and then scramble up through lichens and moss.

The Dog Wall

THE DOG WALL

These routes are located on the cliff band below the north end of the
Little Quarry. The best approach is to climb down the north end of the
obvious gap at the cliff top.

24. **Blodo Manfreak 5.11c** 3 bolts to Metolius rap hangers. A boulder
    problem start leads to an easy traverse across *Too Easy* and then a
    thin technical finish. The difficulty of the crux moves depend largely
    on how tall you are.

25. **Too Easy 5.11d** 5 bolts to standard hangers (1 hanger was miss-
    ing at the time of this writing). A restful start leads to a steep
    traverse on holds that feel like they could explode if you pull too
    hard. Very fun moves.

26. **Beef Man 5.12d** 5 bolts to the *Too Easy* anchors. Climb up *Too
    Easy* to its third bolt and then traverse low along the lip of the big
    roof. Enjoy the powerful pulls with minimal feet.

27. **Traverse of the Dogs 5.11d** (not pictured) Located about 70'
    to the right of *Beef Man*, beginning in the slot to the south of the
    descent gap. This route is an 8 bolt traverse with a couple of mid-
    route Metolius rap hangers for convenient retreat. Unfortunately, at
    the time of this writing, most of the bolt hangers were missing in
    action. Holds on the cliff top are not part of the sequence.

THE BIG TIMES AREA

Some of these boulder problems are kind of tall and might be more enjoyable on toprope.

👍 **28.Short Corner V2** (partially pictured) Stem up the inside corner to a big ledge and then over the top.

29.Two Finger Pocket V3 Start as for *Short Corner* and then traverse over to the pocket and up the face. Look out for Poison Ivy.

30.Undercling to Pocket V5 Direct start to *Two Finger Pocket*. Start with your left hand on the arête and your right hand on the undercling edge. Step up and stab the pocket and then finish as for *Two Finger Pocket*. Look out for Poison Ivy.

31.Corner to Pocket Traverse V0+ Start on *Corner Crack* and then traverse left on a ledge. Finish as for *Two Finger Pocket*.

👍 **32.Hunchback Layback V0-** Stem and lieback up the finger crack in the corner.

👍 **33.Dyno For Dollars V2** Put your foot by your ear and smear up the right-facing lieback feature. This line tends to get coated with dirt every spring, so bring a brush.

The Big Times Area

Michael Stoger floats across **Stoger's Traverse (V7)**.

34.Comfortably Numb V2 Climb straight up on sidepulls and small edges. If you're not tall, you might need a cheater stone to start.

35.Wayback Layback VB This flurry of liebacks and smears is good clean fun for the whole family.

36.Tweak of the Devil V6 Stand up high to a tweaker and then pull through to a big sloper.

37.Project This line will go straight up to the Metolius rap hangers.

38.Stoger's Traverse V7 This problem is an extension of *Big Times*. Traverse from *Wayback Layback* to the end of *Big Times*. Superb!

39.Mini Crack VB Climb up the crack and look for jugs to the left.

40.Big Times V5 Traverse to the right from *Mini Crack* to easy ground around the corner. This problem is reachy and favors tall climbers.

41.Mickey Mantel V0- Start left of the chiseled hold and climb up through the three obvious ledges to a sagebrush mantel.

42.Eaves Drop V7 This problem begins with a hideous undercling and then crosses *Big Times* en route to a lieback above.

43. **Mike's Linkup** **V8** Start as for *Eaves Drop* and then reverse *Stoger's Traverse*. Finish by doing *Tweak of the Devil*.

44. **Sharp Arête** **V3** (not pictured) Climb up the obvious sharp arête without using the large block to the left. There is a bolt at the top for those who prefer the safety of a rope. Look out for Poison Ivy.

45. **Shpofol** **V3** (not pictured) Mantel onto the obvious ledge and stand up. Dyno (a big reach will do if you're tall) for the top.

46. **Slap** **VB** Climb up the slab that faces the main wall.

THE BALCONY (not pictured)
This unquarried boulder is located just down slope from the end of the *Big Times Traverse*. The boulder problems face Boise.

47. **Squatter's Right** **V6** Sit start and traverse the length of the boulder from left to right.

48. **Back Drop** **V6** Sit start at two low crimps and then climb up the center of the wall on good holds.

49. **Slip Fault** **V4** Sit start on an obvious sloper rail to the right of *Back Drop* and then trend left to the *Back Drop* finish.

BOB'S NOSE
There are many linkup possibilities on these routes. An ambitious climber could link all of them without stepping off the rock.

50. **DiscomBOBulator** **V2** Traverse from left to right using handholds on the lip of the roof. Continue beyond the roof until the steep rock runs out. More moves can be added by beginning further to the left.

51. **Bob Down Under** **V1** Sit down start underneath the roof and climb straight out the ceiling and over the top.

52. **Bob Down Under Traverse** **V4** Sit start at the crack at the back of the Bob's Nose "cave". Traverse left on the low slopers to the start of *Bob Down Under*. Finish by doing *Bob Down Under*.

53. **Shish KeBOB** **V6** Start as for *Bob Down Under* and then move out, underneath the roof, to the lower holds of the lip. Traverse to the right on the lip.

Bob's Nose

54. **Bob's Nose V0-** Reach up to jugs on the prow and pull up and over the top.

🤙 55. **Bob's Lower Lip V3** Sit start as for the *Bob Down Under Traverse* and then gain the lip of the roof. Traverse out to the prow and then continue left on the lowest holds of the lip. When these holds run out, merge with the upper traverse and then pull over the top.

56. **Bob the Seal V1** Sit start at the right end of the obvious scoop below the finish of *DiscomBOBulator*. Do one big move to a jug and then do your best seal impression while manteling over the top. "Arh, Arh!" Someone give that seal a fish!

THE BLASTED WALL

It is wise to avoid this wall in the springtime because nesting owls have been known to attack climbers.

57. **Sleeping Dog V0+** Step up to the obvious undercling and pull through to good holds.

58. **Dirt Bag Direct V0-** Step up on a rickety block and lieback to jugs and a dirty mantel. It's a bit reachy.

🤙 59. **Super Crack V2** Ascend the seam to a wild and woolly finish. This problem favors knuckle draggers.

60. Drill Crack V0 Climb up the drill scar to a dirt mantel.

61. Penicillin V2 Barn-door up the left side of the arête.

👍 **62. Claptrap V4** Start on the right side of the arête and slap your way up.

63. Blast Hole VB Climb up the drill scar to a dirt mantel.

64. Pigger Memorial Slab V5 Tiptoe up the slab to two crimps and then lunge for the top. Tall kids will love this one.

👍 **65. The Whole Ordeal V0** Slick sandy rock down low leads to great smearing and stemming up the inside corner.

66. Drilled Pockets V2 Sit start at the lowest drilled pockets. Pull up the arête and then around the corner to a shallow mono.

67. Tubular VB Climb up to the blast hole and over the top.

68. Mantel and Pop V0 Mantel onto the low ledge and go for the top.

69. Boulder Crack V0- Lieback and smear up the inside corner.

70. C & L Route VB Amble up the slab.

The Quarry

71. **Swing Out Sister V1** Lieback up the prominent arête while avoiding a swing into the void.

72. **Crumbling Corner V0-** This inside corner is almost as grungy as it looks. Snapping off a hold could result in quite a ride.

👍 73. **Right Crack V0** Smear up the classic inside corner.

74. **Bomb Bay V0** This rarely climbed jutting groove should be done on toprope. Watch out for poison ivy!

75. **Tom's Corner V3** Smear up the arête on sand ball bearings. There are two pitons at the top for those who are smart enough to toprope.

THE PROPELLER AREA

👍 76. **Matt's Crack 5.10c tr** Ascend the finger crack in the inside corner. Excellent climbing.

77. **Micro Seam 5.11d tr** Start at the left end of the wall and follow the seam up the center of the face. The thin technical moves down low lead to small pockets above.

78. **Shredder 5.11d tr** Wander up the face and into the obvious jam crack.

79. Owl Corner 5.9 tr Climb up the inside corner and over an odd bulge.

80. Nuclear Sunrise 5.12b tr (partially pictured) Start up the obvious left-facing crescent feature and then climb straight up the face.

👍 **81. Nuclear Sunset 5.12a/b tr** (partially pictured) Start as for *Propeller* and then step left into the obvious thin lieback crack. These balancy liebacks will keep you on your toes. This route has been done on lead but it is typically thought of as a toprope problem. There are brand new chain anchors at the top.

👍 **82. Propeller 5.11d tr** (partially pictured) This excellent route ascends the main crack system. Think lieback. Although this route has been done on lead it is typically thought of as a toprope problem. The toprope setup is the same as for *Nuclear Sunset*.

83. It's Not My Corner 5.11a tr (partially pictured) Climb up the prominent corner and diagonal ledge. When the ledge inverts and leans back to the left, continue up this feature. There are anchor bolts over the top.

84. Snake Corner 5.8 (partially pictured) Lieback or stem up the obvious finger crack in the inside corner. There are anchor bolts over the top.

The Quarry

85. **The Center Route 5.7** (partially pictured) Do an awkward mantel and then grovel up the wide groove above. There are anchor bolts over the top.

86. **The Tree Route 5.5** (not pictured) This route goes up the right-facing lieback feature to the right of the large perched tree. There are anchor bolts over the top.

87. **Big Boss Man V5** (not pictured) This pumpy overhanging traverse is located at the back of the *Propeller* corridor, behind a giant rock that leans against the main wall. Traverse to the right on good handholds and minimal feet. Round the corner and continue up the face.

88. **Behind the Boss V0** (not pictured) Traverse from right to left on diagonal edges on the face that faces *Big Boss Man*.

89. **Idiot Proof Traverse V0-** (not pictured) Located across from *The Tree Route* on the backside of the *Peanut Butter Pockets* boulder. Traverse from right to left with your hands on the top of the boulder and your feet on smears.

90. **Peanut Butter Left Arête V0** Slap up the left arête and mantel over the top.

91. **The Grinch V3** Start just left of *Peanut Butter Pockets* at a set of left-facing sidepulls. Climb straight up using nearby *Peanut Butter Pockets* for right-handholds.

92. **Peanut Butter Pockets V2** Climb up the drilled pockets to a big move finale. This problem got its name when someone protested the controversial pockets by filling them with peanut butter.

93. **Peanut Butter Right Arête V0** Scamper up the left side of the right arête and mantel over the top.

94. **Pit Fall VB** (not pictured) Located about 60' down slope from *Peanut Butter Pockets* on a boulder that is perched on top of *Poison Ivy Slab*. Beware of the exposure as you scurry up the west side.

95. **Poison Ivy Slab V0-** (not pictured) Located about 80' down slope from *Peanut Butter Pockets*. There are several ways to ascend this large red slab. The base is infested with poison ivy.

THE ARENA

👍 **96.Moisture Missile 5.11a tr** Start up the crack but then go directly up the face to the bulging corner above. This route can be led but it is typically done on tr. There are hangerless anchor bolts on top.

👍 **97.Misfire 5.11a tr** This route is an alternate start to *Moisture Missile*. Climb up to an obvious ledge and an undercling. A dyno to the left leads to the upper portion of *Moisture Missile*.

98.Colonoscopy 5.13a/b tr Start as for *Moisture Missile* but continue up the right-leaning crack to a bouldery crux finish. Bring your own hangers for the bolts.

👍 **99.Chemotherapy 5.11d tr** Follow the thin crack up the face. There are hangerless anchor bolts over the top.

100. Layback Crack 5.8 Lieback or stem up the inside-corner crack. There are several hangerless anchor bolts over the top.

101.Simon Says 5.11b tr Smear up the slab on the left side of the arête. Be sure to listen for good beta.

102.The Day After 5.11d tr Climb over the right end of the triangular roof and then up the arête above.

The Quarry

Michael Stoger endures the pain of **Colonoscopy (5.13a/b tr)**.

103. Rotten Corner 5.10a tr amble up the inside corner until you are underneath the rotten roof. Don't continue beyond this point.

104. Borrowed Shoes 5.10b tr Smear up the slab and arête. I would recommend using your own shoes.

105. Dirt Corner 5.10a tr A funky start leads to easier climbing. Bring along a good brush and watch for loose chunks.

106. Skinny Flake 5.9 tr What is holding this flake up?

107. Pure Energy 5.11b tr This curvaceous inside corner is pleasantly technical and pumpy.

108. Project This zigzag feature is surprisingly tricky and has not yet been climbed successfully.

109. Henry Barber's Arête 5.12d/5.13a Finesse your way up the arête, past 2 bolts, and then step over to easy ground above the roof. This climb favors taller apes. Bring gear for the top section.

110. Optimator 5.12d/5.13a 4 bolts to Metolius rap hangers. This route ascends the arête section of *Henry Barber's Arête* and then continues up the face directly above.

136

111. **My Own Sandbox 5.13b** 6 bolts to Metolius rap hangers. This route ascends the arête section of *Henry Barber's Arête* and then moves left onto the face passing 4 bolts.

112. **The Aid Roof 5.12d** 3 bolts and supplementary gear. Follow the crack up to the ceiling and then out the left side to easier ground above. Disregard the bolts to the right and on the ceiling.

113. **The Quarry Man 5.12d** 5 bolts to the *Optimator* anchors. Free climb *The Aid Roof* and then merge with *Optimator* above.

114. **Slab Left VB** (not pictured) Smear up the left side of the slab.

115. **Slab Right V0-** (not pictured) Tiptoe up the right side of the slab.

116. **The Naked Edge V1** (see next page) Lieback up the arête.

117. **Night Moves V0** Scamper up the face and onto the slab.

118. **Night Moves Traverse V1** Start on the left side of the block and traverse to the right. Finish over the top.

119. **Night Moves Overhang V1** An awkward mantel over the bulge.

120. **Edging Skills V0** Pick your way up the face of the slab.

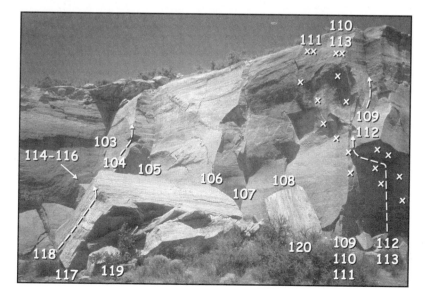

The Quarry

Jesse "SuS" Edmundson opts for garb on **The Naked Edge (V1)**.

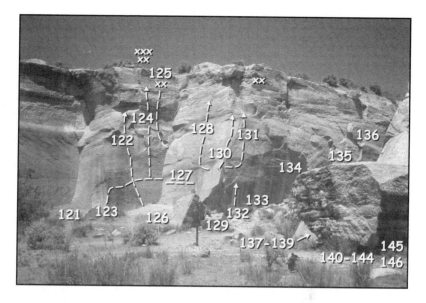

👍 **121. Stem Corner** 5.12a tr Paste your way up the inside corner.

👍 **122. Road Runner** 5.12c tr Climb up the arête on manufactured holds and whatever else you can find.

123. Chiseled Traverse V4 Start at the corner to the left of *Road Runner* and traverse right on the hideous chiseled holds.

124. Another Stoger Route 5.12b tr Climb straight up the face on thin and reachy moves. There are anchor bolts over the top but they have been vandalized.

125. project Start on *Dihedral* and then climb up the face to the chains.

126. Dihedral 5.9+ tr Lieback up the inside corner. The top is usually dirty.

👍 **127. Balance Ledge Traverse** VB Walk the length of the narrow ledge from right to left.

128. Bat Lunge 5.10c tr Start on the ledge above *Bat Crack*. Step left and dyno for an ample jug.

👍 **129. Bat Crack** V0 Lieback up the crack. Recoil in horror if your hand touches something squeaky and furry.

The Quarry

👍 **130. Bat Crack Direct 5.10c tr** Climb up *Bat Crack* and then continue up the arête above.

131. Right of Arête 5.11d tr Climb up *Bat Crack* and then step out right to thin face moves.

132. Bat Face 5.12c tr This line is a direct start to *Right of Arête*. The first step is a doozie!

👍 **133. Pocket Pool 5.11b tr** Stroke your way up the drilled pockets to chains.

134. Pocket Fisherman 5.11c tr Troll for big ones on the right-hand line of drilled pockets. Use the *Pocket Pool* chains.

135. Staircase 5.5 The line ascends the large flake and ledges.

136. Quarry Crack 5.11b tr (partially pictured) This tricky crack is a balancy pumpfest.

THE BOULDERS

137. Under the Table V6 Start under the low roof and traverse right to *Heel Hook*. Continue around the corner and then all the way to *Table Boulder Right Corner*.

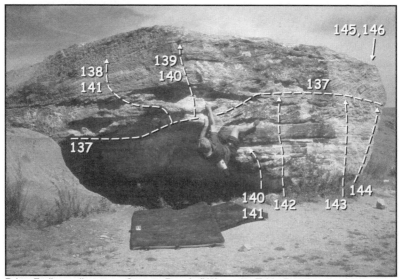

Brian Fedigan clings to a **Sweaty Peach (V2)** on the Table Boulder.

138. **Hook Left** **V2** Reach up to a pair of thin sidepulls and then do an awkward push for the top.

139. **Heel Hook** **V0+** Pull up and over the undercut corner.

140. **The Sweaty Peach** **V2** This is a sit start addition to *Heel Hook*. Begin to the right and slap your way up slopers.

141. **Peaches and Cream** **V4** Start on *The Sweaty Peach* and then traverse into *Hook Left*.

142. **Buckets** **VB** Pull past the big pockets and mantel over the top.

143. **Table Boulder Lunge** **V0** Start at two obvious edges. Paste your feet and pop for the top.

144. **Table Boulder Right Corner** **VB** Climb up the left side of the corner.

145. **Pullover** **V0+** (see picture on page 139) Pull up and over the bulge on the right side of the corner.

146. **Project** (not pictured) Traverse the length of the face from corner to corner without using the top.

147. **Turtle Rock Corner** **5.7 tr** (not pictured) Climb up the obvious inside corner. There are 2 bolts over the top (one is hangerless).

148. **Power Ranger** **5.12c** 5 bolts to the *Crank Cream* chains. The brief flurry of crux moves will have you slapping everywhere but your own back.

149. **Crank Cream** **5.12c** 4 bolts to chains. This route demands strong tendons and good footwork. Don't blow any of the clips!

150. **Popeye Direct** **V0+** Jam up the finger crack to the *Popeye* traverse. Watch out for poison ivy.

151. **Popeye, aka Turtle Rock Traverse** **VB** Traverse the crack under the large overhang.

152. **The Scoop** **V0** Maneuver up the concave face. There are several variations.

The Quarry

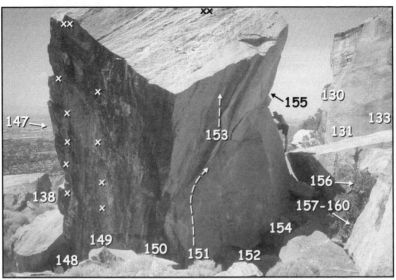

Isaac Madarieta pumps up his forearms on **Popeye (VB)**, Turtle Rock.

153. The Scoop All the Way 5.12a tr Climb up *The Scoop* and then continue up the large overhang. Bring hangers for the anchor bolts.

👍 **154. The Master's Edge V2** Survey the landing before you commit to this touchy lieback up the arête.

155. Never Named 5.10b tr (not pictured) From the highest point on the *Popeye* traverse, climb straight up through the notch. There are 2 old anchor bolts (one is hangerless) near the summit.

156. Behind the Bush V3 (not pictured) Sit start at a right-hand sidepull and a left-hand edge. Pull up the obvious edges.

157. Smoke Me Straight Up V0 (not pictured) The obvious diagonal rail leads to an odd mantel onto the slab.

158. Smoke Me Traverse V0 (not pictured) Start as for *Smoke Me Straight Up* and then traverse up and right along the lip.

👍 **159. Sit Down and Smoke Me V3** (not pictured) Sit down at the base of *Smoke Me Straight Up* and start pulling.

160. Tunnel Traverse V7 (not pictured) This traverse is located in the obvious tunnel to the left of *Smoke Me Straight Up*.

👍 **161. Microman V3** Will your feet to stick as you slap your way up the rounded lieback feature.

162. Right Hand Start V2 Start with your right hand on the obvious edge and climb straight up.

👍 **163. Left Hand Start V0+** Start with your left hand on the obvious edge and climb straight up.

👍 **164. The Crystal V1** Climb up the obvious lieback feature using any holds that you can reach.

👍 **165. The Crystal Butt Start V4** This problem is a sit start addition to *The Crystal*. Start on the right-facing lieback feature and then do a balancy transition into *The Crystal* lieback.

166. Crackerjack V2 Climb up the thin face immediately to the right of *The Crystal*. The final reach is a queasy dyno if you are not tall.

167. Crackerjack Without the Prize V3 Toss aside all common sense and smear up *Crackerjack* without using the "crystal".

👍 **168. Gastons V1** A very big step up leads to the obvious opposing sidepulls and delicate smears.

Bob Meyers tiptoes up **Left Hand Start (V0+)** on the Fortress.

The Quarry

👍 169. **The Fortress Regular Route V0** Start with your right hand on the big edge and climb straight up.

👍 170. **Nick's Problem V0+** Start with both hands on the big edge and step up right to a thin gaston. Match your left foot with your left hand, on the big edge, and go for the top.

171. **The Fortress Right Corner V0+** Think hard about the landing before committing to the crux finish.

👍 172. **The Fortress Traverse V5** Start at the right end of the boulder and traverse all the way left to the *Microman* finish.

173. **The Fortress Edge V2** (not pictured) Lieback up the right side of the arête. Be aware of the landing!

174. **The Fortress Lunge V2** (not pictured) Set up on the small ledge and dyno to the right. Climb to the top.

175. **Great Day for Up! V0+** (not pictured) Sit start, pull up the left arête and mantel over the top. Use the rock that the boulder is perched on for footholds.

176. **Hop on Pop V2** (not pictured) Sit start, pull up the steep side of the right arête and mantel over the top.

photo by Todd Meier, 2000

The author gropes for anything on **Whole Lotta Nothing (5.12b tr)**.

177. California Flake Remains VB After thousands of ascents, northern California has fallen off of California Flake. What remains is a sit start layback problem and a chilling reminder of the power of quarry blasting.

 178. Whole Lotta Nothing 5.12b tr Scamper up the obvious zigzag rails and thin face above. There are 2 aged hangerless bolts over the top.

179. Something of Nothing 5.12c tr Grovel up the right-facing lieback feature to a thin face with small pockets. There are 4 aged hangerless bolts over the top.

180. Pin Scars 5.12d tr Follow the micro seam past evenly spaced pin scars. The starting ledge has disappeared since this climb was established and the opening moves are definitely harder now.

The Quarry

Isaac Madarieta binges on **Kryptonite Hangover (V3)**, Superman Boulder.

SUPERMAN BOULDER

This half-buried boulder is located just below the active quarry site alongside the "Tram Trail". It should be avoided during work hours because of the close proximity to quarry blasting.

181. **Kryptonite Hangover V3** Sit start with your right hand on the "starting hold" and your left hand on a lower edge. Pull through on crimps without using the crack.

182. **Bloody Knuckles V0** Hang from the "starting hold" and then scurry up the crack on jugs.

183. **Lois V1** Hang from the "starting hold" and then traverse right and up without using the crack.

184. **Superman in Reverse V5** Hang from the "starting hold" and then traverse all the way right.

185. **Learning to Fly V4** Start on slopers and grovel to the top on exasperating crimps and more slopers.

186. **Fly By the Seat of Your Pants V5** This is a sit start addition to *Learning to Fly*. Start at the right-facing layback feature and then climb up *Learning to Fly*.

👍 **187. Nice Peace V3** Start as for *Fly By the Seat of Your Pants* but then veer right to sidepulls. Finish up on the left side of the arête.

188. Super Boy V0+ Sit down and then use your superhuman power to fly up the arête.

189. Superman Traverse V6 Start at the right end of the boulder and traverse left without using the *Bloody Knuckles* crack. Finish by doing *Kryptonite Hangover.*

OTHER TABLE ROCK SITES

There are several other bouldering sites in the Table Rock area but they are all located on private land. They are listed here only for their historical relevance as established climbing areas and trespassing is certainly not advised. These sites include the popular *Traverse Wall* on the northeast side of Table Rock and the suburbia enveloped *Conglomerate Cave* on the hillside above Strata Via Way. Others include the *Hillside Caves* that are located about a half mile southeast of the Quarry and the *South Slope*, which is the vast area of boulder strewn slopes and benches (including the Valley of the Trolls) between the Table Rock Quarry and Warm Springs Avenue. One small section of the *South Slope* is actually on public land and it features the top-notch boulder problem, **Red Wall V6**. *Red Wall* is visible down slope from the *Blasted Wall* and it is easy to spot because of its rusty color and triangular shape.

The Boise Bouldering Contest in 1987. The area shown is now actively quarried.

Rocky Canyon

photo by Sandy Epeldi, 1996

Brian Whitney does some fancy footwork on **Twinkle Toes (5.10b)**.

Rocky Canyon has been a site of occasional climbing activity for many years. With its tall rock walls and proximity to Boise, it drew the attention of early climbers. These vertical explorers left behind a handful of routes and a spattering of antique anchor bolts. Despite these pioneering efforts, this small canyon never became a frequent climbing destination because of its generally poor rock quality.

This rock leaves a lot to be desired. The canyon walls are composed mainly of rotten rhyolite and climbing is limited to a few isolated spots where the walls are not a crumbling mess. The established routes are typically on acceptable rock but chunks have been known to come off and caution is always advised. When the rock is sound, it tends to be well-featured and fun to climb.

Possibly the best reason to visit Rocky Canyon is to soak in its history. During the Boise Basin Gold Rush of the 1860s, Rocky Canyon Road (then the "Idaho Road") was the route connecting the Oregon Trail at Boise with the Boise Basin mining camps. Thousands of prospectors flooded into the Boise Basin via this thoroughfare. The road and surrounding landscape have not changed much since that time and old painted advertisements still adorn some of the rock walls.

HOW TO GET THERE

From the intersection of Broadway Ave and Warm Springs Ave, proceed north on Broadway (aka Avenue B) 0.2 mile to Reserve Street. Turn right on Reserve Street and drive about a half mile to Shaw Mountain Road. Turn right onto Shaw Mountain Road (Shaw Mountain Road eventually becomes Rocky Canyon Road) and proceed about 3 miles to Rocky Canyon. The last stretch of road into the canyon is unpaved. Parking can be found at the far end of the canyon. The Bee Block formation is located approximately 0.7 mile further up the canyon.

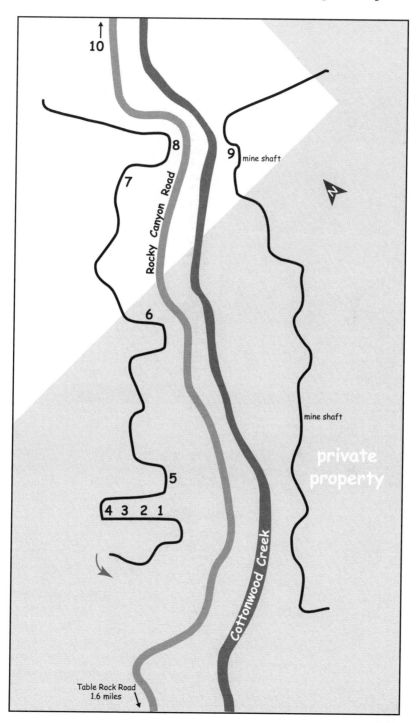

10

8

9   mine shaft

7

N

6

mine shaft

5

private
property

4 3 2 1

Rocky Canyon Road

Cottonwood Creek

Table Rock Road
1.6 miles

Rocky Canyon

Rocky Canyon

Note: Climbs 1-6 are on private property and should probably not be climbed. The area has never been posted (to date) but please respect the landowner's rights.

1. **Lead Foot 5.9** (not pictured) 2 bolts and thin supplementary pro. No anchors. The line starts with a boulder problem directly below the first bolt.

2. **Pioneer Crack 5.6** (not pictured) This route ascends the obvious fracture that splits the wall. The rock quality is uncharacteristically good.

3. **What Crack? 5.11a tr** (not pictured) This elegant line follows the micro seam up the least featured part of the face.

4. **Chimney 5.5** (not pictured) This claustrophobic inside corner feels suspiciously like mountaineering.

5. **The Wagon Rut 5.7** (not pictured) This line is an obvious jam crack that goes up the center of a slab face. The climb ends at a small ledge with an old bolt.

6. **Helen's Pock Marked Face 5.8+ r** (not pictured) This 25' route ascends huecos on a slightly overhanging face with one bolt. There are no anchors and slings are needed to rappel back down.

7. **Twinkle Toes 5.10b** 3 bolts and supplementary pro to Metolius rap hangers. The intended line follows the bolts up the slab. Stay out of the rotten gully to the right!

8. **Roadside Boulder Problem V0** (not pictured) This boulder problem literally starts in the road. Climb up the slippery slab on fun pockets, but watch for cars!

9. **The Old Toll Route 5.7** Ascend the obvious gully and then exit left to a prominent point. Watch out for rotten rock.

10. **The Bee Block 5.6 tr** This 20' bouldering/toprope slab is located right on the road (watch out for cars!) at 0.7 mile up the canyon from *Twinkle Toes*. The rock is granite and the climbing is suitable for novices. Bring an extra-long sling for toprope setup.

Mores Mountain

Roadside Rock (left) and The Pincer (right)

The Mores Mountain area has seen sporadic climbing activity for decades. Traditionally, the climbing experience involved bushwhacking and adventurous crack climbing on crumbling rock. The questionable granite was generally thought of as dirty, rotten, and surprisingly similar to Styrofoam. More than one climber has left the area after a fear-induced pact with God. Despite all of this, a few diehards began looking at the area for sport climbing potential. In July of 1995 a small group of climbers, tired of the unbearable heat in Boise, took refuge in the cool mountain air of Mores Mountain. After several visits and countless hours of scrubbing and cleaning, three routes were established. The first route was the knob snapping *Life Without Beer (5.10b)* followed by the calf burning *Midnight Visitor (5.10b)* and the vicious *Junkie Cosmonaut (5.12c)*. The new climbs were more fun than anticipated and since that time new routes have been established nearly every year.

As mentioned, the rock quality at Mores Mountain is less than pristine but the climbing can be very enjoyable regardless. The routes are mostly technical slabs that are often quite sustained. The footwork is typically smeary if not a little nerve-wracking due to patches of friable granite and a general coating of lichens. The multitudes of knobs and crystals make for great handholds even though they sometimes snap off underfoot. These routes certainly evolve over time as lichens wears away and holds break off. All things considered, the climbing can be surprisingly fun.

THE SEASON

Generally the climbing season runs from May through October. The area is snowed in during the rest of the year.

THE WEATHER

The Mores Mountain crags are situated in a mountain setting at 6600' elevation. This means cooler temperatures and fickle weather. Just because it is 100 degrees in Boise doesn't mean you will be warm up here. Bring a jacket and be prepared for afternoon thunderstorms.

WILDLIFE

This area is swarming with wildlife. Among the animal population are bears and mountain lions. Close encounters with these formidable lurkers are generally uncommon. Still, be aware this is a wild area and use your common sense. Be especially careful during hunting season when the woods are crawling with whiskey-toting Elmer Fudds.

HOW TO GET THERE

The Mores Mountain crags are reached by a 20-mile drive up Bogus Basin Road. From the intersection of Bogus Basin Road and Hill Road, drive north on Bogus Basin Road to the Bogus Creek Lodge at 15.5 miles. Proceed on dirt surface for another 4.5 miles to reach the climbs. En route you will pass the Shafer Butte Picnic Area turnoff (3.3 miles beyond the lodge) where a "road closed" sign is occasionally posted during times of intense logging activity. If so, walk from this point. The climbs are located on the obvious granite outcrops directly above the road. A primitive trail accesses the crags from the far side of the road cut. The trail begins with a brief pull up a fixed line.

photo by Sandy Epeldi, 1995

Hannah North subdues the **Midnight Visitor (5.10b)**.

Mores Mountain

photo by Alex Kittrell, 1997

The author travels **The Long and Winding Road (5.11d)** for the first ascent.

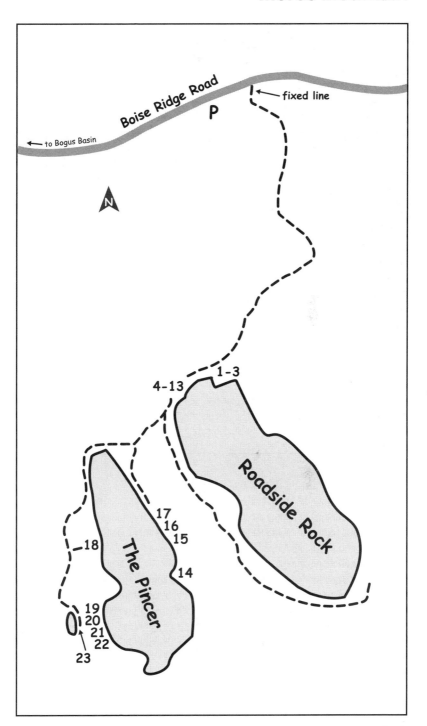

Boise Ridge Road

P

fixed line

← to Bogus Basin

N

4-13

1-3

Roadside Rock

The Pincer

17
16
15

18

14

19
20
21
22

23

Mores Mountain

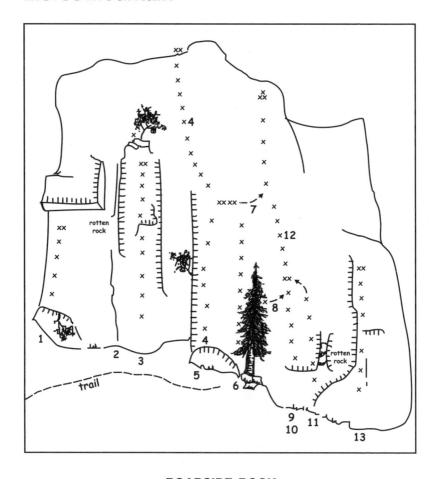

ROADSIDE ROCK

1. **Life Without Beer 5.10b** 4 bolts to Metolius rap hangers. Stickclip the 1st bolt. A cam placement is possible after the 2nd bolt, if desired. The many knobs and crystals are reminiscent of Tuolumne.

2. **Deliverance 5.10a** This grungy crack climb is probably best avoided unless you are an experienced traditional lead climber who doesn't mind getting dirty and scared. The line follows a crack that runs through the right side of the chimney. Finish on the obvious belay ledge at a single bolt and a slingable tree. **Descent:** Rappel from the ledge to avoid extremely rotten rock above.

3. **The Long and Winding Road 5.11d** 9 bolts to Metolius rap hangers. Buckle up and hang on for the ride! The rock is a little crumbly at the crux.

4. Computer Girl 5.9 This route has 2 pitches and a view!
    Pitch #1 5.9 6 bolts to chains. The majority of moves on this pitch are very easy but the crux is devious.
    Pitch #2 5.8 10+ bolts to anchors at the summit. There is a bit of dirty rock on this pitch but it should clean up with traffic. The line meanders a little bit, so bring some long slings to avoid rope drag.
Descent: Walk off the back of the crag. Be careful, it's exposed.

5. Falling Down the Mountain V0 Smear up the face of the boulder below *Computer Girl*. Beware, it's a steep drop off below.

6. Midnight Visitor 5.10b 8 bolts to Metolius rap hangers. A boulder problem start leads to easier but sustained climbing.

7. After Midnight 5.9 This route is an extension of *Midnight Visitor*. From the *Midnight Visitor* anchors, traverse out right to the *Shades of Gray* bolt line. Climb past 4 *Shades of Gray* bolts to Metolius rap hangers.
Descent: Rappel with two ropes or do two rappels using the *Midnight Visitor* anchors for the second rappel.

8. Heart of Darkness 5.10b 15 bolts to anchors. This route is a link up of *Midnight Visitor*, *Junkie Cosmonaut* and *Shades of Gray*. Start on *Midnight Visitor* and climb to its 3rd bolt. Traverse to the right past a single bolt and merge with *Junkie Cosmonaut*. Climb past 1 bolt on *Junkie Cosmonaut* en route to the *Junkie Cosmonaut* anchors. Now climb *Shades of Gray*. **Descent:** 2 rope rappel.

9. Junkie Cosmonaut 5.12c 5 bolts to Metolius rap hangers. Stick-clip the 1st bolt. The powerful crux moves are at the bulge below the 1st bolt and basically amount to a boulder problem on toprope. The rest of the route consists of delicate slab moves.

10. Garnet Fever 5.11b A0 This variation of *Junkie Cosmonaut* eliminates the 5.12 moves. Hoist yourself up the rope to the 1st bolt of *Junkie Cosmonaut*. Climb the rest of the route free. The moves are very delicate and balancy. This climb used to be easier but some key holds have broken off.

11. Freaky Toy Girl 5.10d 5 bolts to the *Junkie Cosmonaut* anchors. Follow the bolt line closely past the first 3 bolts to avoid rotten rock to the right. Definitely don't stem out right.

Mores Mountain

Pete Pollard sidles up **Back Slide (5.10a/b)** with The Pincer in the background.

👍 **12. Shades of Gray 5.10b** This route begins at the anchors of *Junkie Cosmonaut* and ascends past 9 bolts to Metolius rap hangers. It can be used as an extension of *Junkie Cosmonaut*, *Garnet Fever* or *Freaky Toy Girl*. From the ground, this is a very long pitch that requires a minimum of 17 quick draws. **Descent:** 2 rope rappel.

13. Back Slide 5.10a/b 6 bolts to Metolius rap hangers. Have you ever used chimney technique on a sport climb?

THE PINCER - East Face

14. Snapper 5.7 6 bolts to Metolius rap hangers. This route is located high up on the Pincer. It ascends the slab to the left of the prominent left-leaning open book. An exposed scramble is necessary to reach the saddle where the climb begins.

👎 **15. Leslie's Dirty Crack 5.9 r** This line ascends the obvious rotten crack to the left of *The Cat's Pajamas* and ends at *The Cat's Pajamas* anchors. You can clip the upper bolts of *The Cat's Pajamas* if exfoliating rock and lousy protection are not your cup of tea.

16. The Cat's Pajamas 5.10d 5 bolts to Metolius rap hangers. A crumbly boulder problem start leads to exfoliating rock above. Hopefully this line cleans up with traffic.

👍 **17. Daisy-Head Mayzie 5.12a** 5 bolts to *The Cat's Pajamas* anchors. A funkedelic crux start leads to fun layback moves above. Hopefully the small edge below the 2nd bolt doesn't snap off!

THE PINCER - West Face

18. The Butt Start Boys 5.11a (not pictured) 3 bolts to chains on a short arête. Some may feel compelled to sit start.

19. Open Project Only the anchors have been installed so far.

20. Tool Boys 5.10b 9 bolts to the *Stepping Razor* anchors. The route merges with *Stepping Razor* after the seventh bolt. Use a 60-meter rope.

👍 **21. Stepping Razor 5.11c** 7 bolts to anchors consisting of a single chain and a cold shut. Tiptoe directly up the bolt line on the delicate slab. It's a calf-burning classic.

Mores Mountain

22. Brand-new Secondhand 5.10b This line is a wandering variation of *Stepping Razor*. Stickclip the first bolt and then climb up the crystal-laden dike to bypass the difficult moves. Join *Stepping Razor* at the 3rd bolt. Expect reachy clips!

23. Green-eyed Bugs V0 This boulder problem is located on a small rock that faces the previously described routes. Step up to the rail at the obvious diagonal dike and traverse uphill until you can step off the rock.

Isaac Madarieta cleans up his route, **Stepping Razor (5.11c)**, on The Pincer.

OTHER CRAGS IN THE AREA

There are many other granite outcrops in the Mores Mountain/Bogus Basin area. A lot of them have established climbs but the rock is usually dirty and often questionable. The most impressive of these features is Castle Rock with its 400' north face. For more information about the area's outcrops consult a forest service map or a USGS quadrangle.

BUFFALO ROCK

This small granite outcrop is located right next to Bogus Basin Road at about 8.5 miles up the road from Hill Road. It is worth checking out if you have already climbed everything else in Boise. This crag is on private property so be respectful of the owner's rights and don't trespass if a sign is posted. The routes are listed below in clockwise order from the road. Bring cams and slings to backup the aged anchor bolts.

1. **Easy Cracks 5.6** Climb up the obvious cracks just right of *Buffalo Slab Right.*

2. **Buffalo Slab Right 5.9 tr** Run up the slab past 2 hangerless bolts.

3. **Buffalo Slab Left 5.10a tr** Paste your way up the slab past 2 hangerless bolts.

4. **Buffalo Crack 5.12a tr** Grovel up the overhanging diagonal crack at the downhill end of the boulder. Go right when the crack peters out or continue straight up for a 5.12d direct variation.

5. **Buffalo Arête 5.11b tr** Pull past 2 hangerless bolts on the surprisingly fun overhanging face to the left of the arête. This climb is so ridiculously short that youngsters will be looking for a sit start.

13 MILE BOULDERS

These two boulders are located about 13.5 miles up Bogus Basin Road from Hill Road. They are visible above the road shortly before the Doe Point turnoff. The first boulder (Superman Boulder) has two 20' crack climbs that are described below. The second boulder (Atomic Boulder) is a perched granite ball that will certainly relinquish stout boulder problems to an adventurous soul with a sturdy wire brush.

1. **Easy Thirteen 5.8** Climb up the grungy crack that faces the road.

2. **Superman Crack 5.11b** Jam up the overhanging crack to chains.

Swan Falls

The Black Slabbath Area, just one of the many boulder clusters at Swan Falls.

Located in the Snake River Canyon, a mere 45 minutes from downtown Boise, is a premier bouldering area known as Swan Falls. This unique boulder strewn landscape has been likened to some of North America's top bouldering sites. The area is home to literally thousands of well-featured basalt boulders and the rock quality is impeccable. Boulder problems abound at all degrees of difficulty and range in character from short dalliances to highball mindbenders.

Boise area climbers have been playing on the Swan Falls boulders for many years, but it wasn't until 1998 that the site truly blossomed as a bouldering area. That season, Boise climbers Chris Parker, Scott Bernstrom, and Jeff Smith made a systematic sweep of the area: exploring all of the boulders, climbing them, cleaning them, and leaving behind a wake of challenging boulder problems. Other locals such as Michael Stoger and Dale Snyder contributed with a number of difficult problems, such as Mike's outstanding test piece traverse, *Power Trip (V9)*, on the backside of Burnt Boulder.

The story of Swan Falls bouldering actually begins about 14,300 years ago when the Bonneville Flood rushed through the Snake River Canyon. This violent deluge tore large pieces of basalt from the canyon walls and tumbled them along with the current. The tumbling action rounded, polished, and redeposited the basalt pieces as tailor made boulders perfectly suited for climbing.

The character of Swan Falls bouldering is a direct product of the boulders' flood origins. The water tumbled boulders are generally rounded

Swan Falls

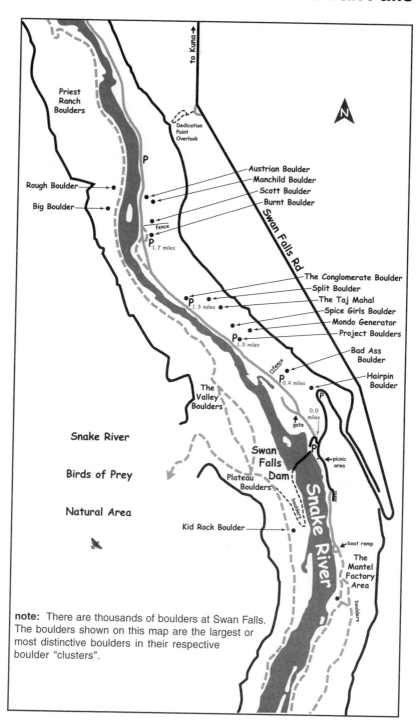

note: There are thousands of boulders at Swan Falls. The boulders shown on this map are the largest or most distinctive boulders in their respective boulder "clusters".

Swan Falls

photo by Dan Smith, 2001

Jeff Smith climbs up the charts on **Going Platinum (V4)**, Kid Rock Boulder.

in shape making for steep undercut starts and wild finishing mantels. The water polished surface means that handholds can be real power drainers and footholds are often insecure and smeary. The combination of these elements makes Swan Falls bouldering uniquely challenging, powerful, and fun.

THE SEASON

Bouldering is possible at Swan Falls year-round. The optimum times are spring and fall when the temperatures are mild. In the summer, morning temps are okay but the rest of the day is definitely too hot. During the winter, the canyon walls provide some shelter from the elements and the temp can be surprisingly comfortable.

THE SNAKE RIVER BIRDS OF PREY NATURAL AREA

Swan Falls is located within the Snake River Birds of Prey Natural Area. Established in 1971, this natural area was set aside to protect the densest nesting population of raptors in the world. Visitors to the area are treated to views of these majestic birds soaring above the canyon rim. Resident raptors include golden eagles, prairie falcons, red-tailed hawks, ferruginous hawks, and many more. The best time for viewing is from February to June.

Please tread lightly in the Snake River Birds of Prey Natural Area and never do anything that might disturb the raptors. First and foremost, do not climb on or near the canyon walls (the rock is lousy any-

Swan Falls

way) because this is where the raptors nest and they are very sensitive to human presence. Climbers should familiarize themselves with all of the area's posted rules and abide by them. This will help to preserve the birds of prey as well as our continued access to the area.

SWAN FALLS DAM

Named for the swans that once wintered in the vicinity, Swan Falls Dam was the first dam on the Snake River. Built in 1901, the dam's purpose was to provide power to the booming mining operations at Silver City. This objective was accomplished at the expense of the river's steelhead and Chinook salmon runs, which were blocked by the dam and effectively ended. The dam is still operational today and tours are available for those who are turned on by turbines.

HOW TO GET THERE

To reach Swan Falls, drive west from Boise on I-84 and take the Meridian/Kuna exit (exit 44). Turn left (south) on Kuna-Meridian Road (State Route 69) and proceed forward about 8 miles to the outskirts of Kuna where the road curves right and becomes Avalon Road. Proceed on Avalon Road for about a mile to Swan Falls Road. Turn left on Swan Falls Road and travel about 20 miles to Swan Falls Dam. From this point, refer to the overview map for details on how to find specific bouldering sites. Access to the west side of the river is afforded by walking across the dam.

Will Nesse clings to the Taj Mahal Boulder with Split Boulder in the background.

Other Climbing Areas - North

THE GARDEN VALLEY AREA

In the Garden Valley area, about an hour drive from Boise, there are numerous granite outcrops. They are scattered throughout the area with the highest concentration of rock in the Silver Creek drainage. Some of these crags have established climbs but most are somewhat remote and have not been developed. The climbing generally requires a sense of adventure and a sturdy pair of hiking boots. One crag that is easily accessible is right by the road but it only offers a couple of climbs. To reach this particular crag, drive north on Hwy-55 to Banks and then turn right on the road to Garden Valley. Drive about 3.5 more miles and look for the crag on the hillside above.

THE NEEDLES

Near the small town of Donnelly, some granite spires are visible on the ridgetop to the east. This cluster of crags (The Needles), which has been dubbed "No Tellum" by its developers, sports more than 75 routes. The rock is rumored to be of reasonably good quality and the climbing has been described as "slabby". Accessing these remote mountain crags involves navigating a maze of tedious forest service roads that branch out from Gold Fork Road (FS Rd #498). Use a Boise National Forest map and the USGS Gold Fork Rock quadrangle to find your way. The drive from Boise can take nearly 3 hours and the area's climbing season runs from late spring through October.

photo by Sarah Brandenberger, 2001

A small sampling of the many Needles Crags.

Jug Handle Mountain is not your neighborhood climbing gym.

THE MCCALL AREA

The mountains around McCall offer backcountry climbing on granite. The area is not Yosemite Valley but there are a few established routes worth checking out. The most popular climb in the area is the 10-pitch *Triple Cracks (5.6)* on Slick Rock. This route looms above Lick Creek Road and is hard to miss. The Lick Creek area is also rumored to sport decent bouldering for those who are willing to drive three hours to boulder.

Climbing in McCall is not limited to Slick Rock and a few obscure boulder problems. There are mountains in the area that sport impressive walls. One example is Jug Handle Mountain. During the 2002 season, the Northeast Face of Jug Handle Mountain saw quite a bit of activity. Michael Stoger and Jeff Smith established two 4-pitch routes (5.10a and 5.10d) and Mike later returned to establish the 3-pitch *Dream Catcher (5.12d/5.13a)*. For information about other mountains in the area refer to Tom Lopez's book, "Idaho: A Climbing Guide". To reach the McCall area from Boise, drive north on Hwy-55. It takes about two hours to reach McCall and then the climbing is further out on various forest service roads. Bring along a forest service map for specific details.

RIGGINS LIMESTONE

This excellent sport climbing area is located in the Seven Devils Mountains near the town of Riggins. The site features about 100 steep and physically challenging routes on quality limestone. Despite the

Other Climbing Areas - North

area's sandbag reputation, there are actually climbs for just about everyone, ranging from 5.9 to impossible. To reach the area, take Hwy-55 to New Meadows and then Hwy-95 almost to Riggins. About a quarter mile before Riggins, turn left on the dirt surface Squaw Creek Road. There is a sign marking this intersection that reads, "Seven Devils Campground 17 miles". The crags are located about 10 miles up this road. The drive from Boise takes about three and a half hours. For more information refer to the book "Riggins Limestone" by yours truly.

HELLS CANYON

Hells Canyon, located about three hours north of Boise, is an excellent limestone sport climbing area with more routes than you can shake your stickclip at. There are literally hundreds of routes in the area covering the whole spectrum of difficulty. There are delicate slabs, steep cave routes, and everything in between. The climbing is so fun that you might forget about the rattlesnakes and poison ivy.

To reach the Hells Canyon Limestone from Boise, drive west on I-84 to the Fruitland exit and Hwy-95. Proceed north on Hwy-95 to Cambridge and then turn left on State Route-71. Drive north on State Route-71 past Brownlee Reservoir and Oxbow Reservoir to Hells Canyon Reservoir. As you drive along the reservoir, look for the obvious band of gray limestone that cuts through the Canyon's typical dark rock. This is where the climbing is located. It is about ten miles before the road's end at Hells Canyon Dam. Most of the routes are located in the Allison Creek, Little Dry Gulch and Eckels Creek drainages. Primitive camping is located on Big Bar just below the climbing area. The season runs from fall through spring. Summers are hot as Hades.

Two of the many limestone crags in Hells Canyon.

photo by Sandy Epeldi, 1997

Alex Kittrell on **The Sunrise Book (5.12a)**, The Elephant Perch.

ARROWROCK RESERVOIR

During the spring of 2001, a small cluster of granite crags above Arrowrock Reservoir became the focus of some minor route development. One 5.10 route was established and a project line received anchors. A few boulder problems were also done. The rock quality is said to be similar to the rock at Mores Mountain and apparently the area is ripe for more routes and boulder problems. To reach these crags from Boise, drive east on Hwy-21 to the large bridge that spans Lucky Peak Reservoir. After crossing the bridge, turn right on Forest Service Road #268 (the road to Atlanta) and proceed about 13 miles, passing Arrowrock Dam en route, to the crags. The outcrops are easily seen uphill from the road and the approach is short. The drive takes less than an hour.

THE SAWTOOTH MOUNTAINS

The much-ballyhooed Sawtooth Mountains used to be Idaho's secret Yosemite. These days you can meet climbers from all over the country at the area's premier crag, The Elephant Perch. Despite the Sawtooths' increasing popularity, solitude is still not difficult to find in the area's endless granite. For general information about Sawtooth climbing, refer to Tom Lopez's book, "Idaho: A Climbing Guide". The Sawtooths are located about three hours from Boise via Hwy-21.

Other Climbing Areas - East

BLUE GILL

Blue Gill, located about two hours southeast of Boise, is a fun alternative to the more popular climbing areas in the region. This sleepy little crag offers nearly fifty routes ranging from 5.6 to 5.11. The rock is non-columnar basalt with many cracks and a few bolted faces. Unfortunately, rumors have circulated that these crags might be unstable. You might want to inquire locally before roping up. Refer to Mark Weber's guidebook, "Basalt Climbs of South-Central Idaho" for more information.

To reach Blue Gill from Boise, take I-84 to the Hwy-30 exit near Gooding. Head south on Hwy-30 almost to Buhl. Turn right on 4200 North at a point where the highway turns left toward Buhl near the Black Bear Tavern. Proceed two miles on 4200 North and then turn right on 900 East. Drive one tenth of a mile on 900 East and then turn left onto a gravel road. Proceed about one mile on the gravel road and then turn right on a primitive dirt road. Drive another two tenths of a mile to a wide parking area. Walk a short distance north, crossing a couple of fences, to the climbing area. The climbing season is basically the same as Boise's.

DIERKES LAKE

This versatile climbing area is located about two hours from Boise on the outskirts of Twin Falls. It offers steep sport climbs, traditional crack climbs, and a plentitude of bouldering. The rock is basalt and it is typically steep and well featured. One Dierkes climber told me that a particularly steep route in "The Alcove" has "the biggest holds on Earth". The best time to climb at Dierkes is spring or fall but it is possible to climb year round if you don't mind scorching summer heat and frigid winter cold.

To reach Dierkes Lake from Boise, take I-84 east to the Twin Falls exit. Take the exit, which will put you on Blue Lakes Blvd, and drive into Twin Falls. Proceed on Blue Lakes Blvd to its intersection with Falls Ave and then turn left. Proceed on Falls Ave for about 3 miles and then turn left on Champlin Rd. Proceed on Champlin Rd to the Shoshone Falls/ Dierkes Lake Park Complex where you will be charged a small entrance fee. For more information about Dierkes Lake and other Twin Falls area crags, refer to Mark Weber's guidebook, "Basalt Climbs of South-Central Idaho" and "Rock and Ice Magazine", issue #56.

THE LAVA CAVES

Near the Shoshone Ice Caves are two lava tubes that offer a handful of exceptionally steep jug-infested routes from 5.10c to 5.13b. To reach this area from Boise, drive east on I-84 to Gooding and then take Hwy-26 to Shoshone. Turn left at Shoshone, onto Hwy-75, and proceed to the Shoshone Ice Caves. Access the smaller of the two lava tubes (The Little Cave) by turning right at the Shoshone Ice Caves gift shop and driving a very short distance to a pullout on the right. Park and walk south for a short distance to the collapsed cave. To reach the larger lava tube (The Snake Pit) from Hwy-75, turn right on Burmah Road shortly before the turnoff to the Shoshone Ice Caves. Drive about a half-mile to a dirt road on the left. Follow the dirt road to the fourth telephone pole and park. Walk toward the highway (west) for a couple of hundred yards to the collapsed cave. The drive takes about two and a half hours.

THE CITY OF ROCKS

Everyone who has ever squeezed into a pair of climbing shoes has heard of the City of Rocks. This world class climbing area offers hundreds of routes for sport climbers and trad climbers alike. To get there from Boise take I-84 east to Burley and then State Route-27 south to Oakley. At Oakley turn left and follow signs to the City of Rocks. The drive takes about three hours. The season runs from spring through fall. Refer to Dave Bingham's "City of Rocks: A Climber's Guide" for specific details.

MASSACRE ROCKS STATE PARK

Spend a weekend at Massacre Rocks and you might fall in love. You'll be tagged as a petrosexual and shunned from your community. Seriously though, with over 600 routes and a generous spattering of bolts, how can you go wrong. There are routes here for everyone no matter what level they climb. The rock is non-columnar basalt and the climbs tend to be conveniently clustered side-by-side along various walls. The area is so user-friendly that a couple of climbers have ascended more than one hundred routes in a single day. For all the specifics, refer to the free online Massacre Rocks guidebook on the Idaho State University website (www.isu.edu/outdoor/climbing/massacre.htm).

Massacre Rocks State Park is located about three hours from Boise, alongside I-86, near American Falls. The climbs are located on the opposite side of the Snake River from the park facility. The easiest access to the climbing is afforded by a canoe ride across the river. If you don't have a canoe, it is necessary to drive past the park and cross to the north side of the river at American Falls Dam. This approach takes more than four hours and is somewhat difficult to navigate. It is also subject to change. Check the Idaho State University website for current information. Camping is posh and spendy at the park facility but primitive and free on the north side of the river. The climbing season is roughly the same as Boise's.

Other Climbing Areas - East

photo by Sandy Epeldi, 2001

Brian Fedigan climbs **A Face in the Crowd (5.10b)** at Massacre Rocks.

ROSS PARK

Ross Park is a Pocatello city park that just happens to have a climbing area in addition to the playground, picnic area, and zoo. This park sports dozens of short but fun climbs on well-featured basalt cliffs. Most of the routes are toprope problems but there are also lead climbs for the ambitious and park benches for the uninspired. Every September, the Pocatello Pump is held at this site and it is a highly recommended event. Pocatello is less than four hours east of Boise via I-84 and I-86.

Other Climbing Areas - South

THE PEACH BOULDER

During the spring of 2003, Michael Stoger established some challenging boulder problems on a boulder near Windy Point in the Owyhee Desert. The Peach Boulder, as it has become known, offers some of the most difficult bouldering in the Boise area. To reach The Peach Boulder, drive south from Nampa on Hwy-45 to the Snake River and Walters Ferry. Turn left on Hwy-78 and proceed 0.7 mile to Upper Reynolds Creek Road. Drive up Upper Reynolds Creek Road for about 5 miles to the second of two small canyons on the right-hand side of the road (these canyons are within close proximity of each other and both have an ATV trailhead.). Turn toward the canyon on a short dirt road, which will take you to parking and the trailhead. Walk the left-hand fork of the trail into the canyon for about five minutes to the very obvious Peach Boulder. The drive from Boise takes about fifty minutes.

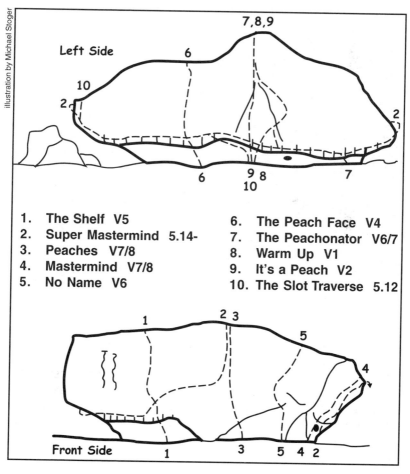

illustration by Michael Stoger

1. **The Shelf V5**
2. **Super Mastermind 5.14-**
3. **Peaches V7/8**
4. **Mastermind V7/8**
5. **No Name V6**
6. **The Peach Face V4**
7. **The Peachonator V6/7**
8. **Warm Up V1**
9. **It's a Peach V2**
10. **The Slot Traverse 5.12**

Other Climbing Areas - South

WINDY POINT BOULDERS

This boulder-strewn hillside offers a pleasant alternative to other Boise area bouldering. The scattered granite boulders are home to numerous established problems from V0 to V8. Projects as hard as V10 are also in the works due to the vision of bouldering guru Mike McClure. The boulders are a bit spread out but the main area is at the pass just before the cattle guard. To reach the area, drive south from Nampa on Hwy-45 to the Snake River and Walters Ferry. Turn left on Hwy-78 and proceed 0.7 mile to Upper Reynolds Creek Road. Turn right on Upper Reynolds Creek Road and drive 10 miles to the Windy Point Boulders. They will be on the left side of the road and you can't miss them. The drive from Boise takes approximately one hour.

POINT OF ROCKS

Point of Rocks is a cluster of granite outcrops that look more inviting from a distance than they do up close. The rocks tend to be too tall for bouldering but too short to warrant uncoiling a rope. There are short crack climbs of the rarely-done grungy variety and short faces awaiting bolts. Boulderers might find something to clean. This is a project for future generations. To travel into this future, drive south from Nampa on Hwy-45 to the Snake River and Walters Ferry. Turn left on Hwy-78 and drive about 9.5 miles to Murphy. Turn right on Old Hwy-45 Street to Murphy Reynolds Stage Road. Drive 1 mile on Murphy Reynolds Stage Road and then turn left on Old Stage Road #37126 (toward Silver City). Drive 5 miles on the rugged Old Stage Road, to a point where a well facility is visible to the left, and then turn right on road #3375. Drive 1.5 miles to the obvious crags. The drive takes about an hour and fifteen minutes from Boise.

RABBIT CREEK CRAGS

This crag-studded ridgeline has an abundance of granite that beckons from across the desert floor. Up close the outcrops are smaller than expected and the angles can be less than inspiring. The good news is that the rock quality is reasonably good and a few toprope lines have been established. There are also rumors about some sport climbs in the area, but I didn't see a single bolt when I visited. One wall stands out as more promising than the rest and it offers up some obvious lines for the future. It is located on the west side of the outcrops and can be reached via a mile-long hike over the ridge.

To reach these Crags, drive south from Nampa on Hwy-45 to the Snake River and Walters Ferry. Turn left on Hwy-78 and drive about 9.5 miles to Murphy. Turn right on Old Hwy-45 St to Murphy Reynolds Stage Road. Drive 6 miles on Murphy Reynolds Stage Road and then

An uncharacteristically large outcrop at the Rabbit Creek Crags.

turn left on the rugged road #37127—from here the crags loom above. Drive your high clearance vehicle up this jeep track to a right hand turn onto an even more rugged track at 2.2 miles. Follow this track for 0.1 mile to an unmarked trailhead. Use this trail to access the ridgeline and crags. The drive from Boise takes about an hour and fifteen minutes.

SILVER CITY

Anyone who has ever visited the historic gold rush town of Silver City has certainly noticed that there are many granite outcrops in the area. Most of the rock is concentrated around New York Summit but the largest and arguably most impressive crag is on the hillside above the town site. These crags have seen sporadic climbing activity over the years and rumors abound about established routes with fixed anchors. For the most part however, the area is still a blank canvas. To reach Silver City, drive south from Nampa on Hwy-45 to the Snake River and Walters Ferry. Turn left on Hwy-78 and proceed about 14 miles to Silver City Road. Turn right on Silver City Road and proceed about 19.5 miles up the windy steep road to New York Summit and Silver City. The drive from Boise takes about an hour and forty-five minutes. The road is snowbound during the winter.

Other Climbing Areas - West

JUMP CREEK CANYON

Jump Creek Canyon is a popular day hike area that also sports a couple of bouldering caves. These caves are located within a stone's throw of the trailhead, on the opposite side of the creek. The rock is rhyolite and the boulder problems are of the steep and vicious variety. Avoid the bolted sport route in the big cave because it is has a dangerous loose block. To reach Jump Creek Canyon, drive west from Nampa on Hwy-55 to Marsing. Continue past Marsing for a couple of miles to where Hwy-55 intersects with Hwy-95. Turn left on Hwy-95 and drive a couple of miles to Poison Creek Road. Turn right on Poison Creek Road and then navigate past a few private lanes to a dirt road that accesses Jump Creek Canyon. The canyon is clearly visible from the road and is easy to get to. The drive from Boise takes about forty-five minutes.

LESLIE GULCH

Leslie Gulch is a strikingly aesthetic vastness of volcanic tuff towers in the Mahogany Mountains of southeastern Oregon. The rock is similar to, but not as solid as, the volcanic tuff at Smith Rock. There are more than 80 established routes at Leslie Gulch. The majority of these routes are sport climbs but there are also some crack climbs. *The Windy Tower (5.11a)* is an outstanding crack climb that can be seen on the right side of the road as you approach the Einstein parking area. The sport routes are clustered on the Einstein wall, the Asylum wall, and throughout Dago Gulch. For more information refer to Sport Climbing Magazine Vol. 3, no. 3.

Unfortunately, Leslie Gulch has been a focal point of controversy for many years. The infamous manufactured routes on the Einstein and Asylum were responsible for a moratorium on route development and BLM plans for bolt removal. Access remains tenuous but so far the bolts remain and climbing has been allowed to continue. If climbing on drilled pockets is not for you, skip the Einstein and Asylum and head straight to the natural sport routes in Dago Gulch.

The drive from Boise to Leslie Gulch takes about an hour and forty-five minutes. From Boise, take I-84 to Nampa and then access Hwy-55 via the sugar plant exit. Head west on Hwy-55 through Marsing and then on to a junction with Hwy-95. Turn left onto Hwy-95 and drive about 20 miles south to McBride Creek Road (marked by a Leslie Gulch sign). Turn right on the dirt surfaced McBride Creek Road and proceed, following the Leslie Gulch signs, about 25 miles to Leslie Gulch. The approach to the Einstein and Asylum begins at a small pullout, by a cattle guard, near the Leslie Gulch ranger hut. The Asylum is the giant flower petal shaped tower looming above the road and it is approached via the trail up Leslie Gulch. Hike about a quarter mile up Leslie Gulch and look for a trail that veers off right and up to the Asylum. The Einstein is a little further up the Leslie Gulch trail and you can't miss it. Dago Gulch is slightly further down the road from the pullout, by the ranger hut. There are primitive campsites at Dago Gulch. The climbing season at Leslie Gulch is the same as Boise's.

BURNT RIVER

Near the tiny town of Durkee (not Dierkes), Oregon, about 2 hours from Boise, is nestled an outstanding band of limestone on the banks of the less than mighty Burnt River. These crags are home to approximately 50 sport routes with potential for many more. Many of the area's routes are located right along the roadside—affording easy access—but the densest concentration of routes is in the ironically named "French Gulch". The nature of the climbing is typically steep and powerful but there are also some delicate slab routes to make your brain hum. The climbing season is more or less the same as Boise's.

To reach Burnt River from Boise, drive about 94 miles west on I-84, past Ontario, to Durkee (20 some miles east of Baker). From the Durkee exit, drive about a half-mile through town to a T-intersection. Turn right on Old Highway-13 and drive 1.5 miles to an intersection with Burnt River Canyon Road. Turn left and drive 12 miles on the Burnt River Canyon Road, passing the Lost Dutchman Mining Association en route, to the Burnt River Crags. You will know that you have arrived when the barren hillsides give way to limestone towers. There is private property in this area so try to keep a low profile and be respectful of the landowners' rights.

SPRING MOUNTAIN

Although Spring Mountain is a long way from the Boise area (about 4 hours), it is worth checking out. The crag is a one hundred foot tall and quarter mile long andesite cliff with unique porous, knobby rock. It offers a mix of more than one hundred sport and trad routes ranging from 5.4 to 5.12. Southern alignment means lots of sunshine but the 4600' elevation means that winters are out. To reach the area from Boise, drive west on I-84 to LaGrande, Oregon. Continue 19 miles beyond LaGrande to the "Summit Road Mt. Emily exit" (exit 243). Turn right and proceed about 9 miles on this gravel road to where a sign reads "Whitman Route Overlook". Turn left at the sign and drive about a mile to a meadow where a gravel road cuts off to the right. Follow the gravel road a short distance to its end at some boulders. Park and walk into the crag. Specific route information can be accessed via the Whitman College website.

First Ascents

Tedd Thompson spreads his wings on the first ascent of **Flight 1713 (5.11c)**.

First Ascents

This first ascent list does not adequately reflect the contributions of Boise's pioneering climbers from the late 1960s through the late 1970s. These intrepid climbers played a formative role in the development of Boise climbing by scaling countless virgin lines and establishing many of the area's classic routes. Unfortunately, few of these ascents were ever documented. As a result, many of this era's first ascents are unknown. Listed here are some of the climbers who established routes during these significant years in Boise climbing: Bob Allen, Brad Beaver, Mike Blackaller, Al Botticelli, Bob Boyles, Rick Braun, Bill Burns, Charlie Crist, Barry DeWane, Tony Engleman, Frank Florence, Bob Henry, Bob Jahn, Craig Malone, Dan McHale, John McLeod, Tom McLeod, Nick Meyers, Tom Naylor, Curtis Olson, John Platt, John Rozell, Rick Rozell, Ron Sargent, Art Troutner, Mike Weber, Joel Weinberg, Ray York.

FIRST ASCENT KEY

First Ascent - The first successful ascent of a route on lead, in other words, the first redpoint ascent. Many of these routes had aid ascents or toprope ascents prior to the "first ascent".

1st TR - The first successful toprope ascent of a route.

REB - Route Engineered By... This is the person who committed the time and resources to put up the route (bolting, cleaning, etc). "REB" is only listed when the first ascent climber is not the person who equipped the route prior to the 1st ascent.

_♪_ - This route was originally a traditional gear route but it has been retro-bolted and converted into a sport route. The first ascent was done without bolts.

_⌒_ - This route has been partially retro-bolted since the first ascent. At least one bolt has been added to the original protection.

_ρ_ - This route was originally protected with pitons in addition to traditional gear placements.

_N_ - This route was not named by the first ascent party. The route was named later by someone else. Climbers of the 1970's, more often than not, didn't name the climbs they did.

_☀_ - This route was destroyed by quarry blasting.

Note: First ascent lists are prone to error. Obviously, first ascents can be difficult, if not impossible, to pin down. The following list reflects the earliest ascents that were reported to me during the making of this book.

_N_ 409 5.8... Mike Weber, Bob Boyles - circa 1978
After Midnight 5.9.............................. Sandy Epeldi, Ben Smith, Matt Fritz - 7/99
Aid Roof, The 5.12d........................ Michael Stoger - 1999; 1st aid: Ray York - 1967
_N ♪_ Ajax 5.9.. unknown
All the Way Home 5.10a.................. Steve Fransen, J. Aguinaga, Kate Cahill - 1997
Allison Wonderland 5.10c................ Todd Montgomery, Tedd Thompson, Steve
                                                   Fransen, Almer Casile, Allison Frisbee - 1995
Almer Casile Mem. Buttress 5.8....... Todd Montgomery - circa 1997
Ambition is Critical 5.10b.................. Nathan Jensen, Taylor Jensen - 1999
Angry Bunnies 5.10c........................ Steve Fransen, Kate Cahill, Jacob Sack - 1997
Another Face in the Crowd 5.11c/d.. Matt Fritz - circa 1988
_N_ Another Stoger Route 5.12b tr......... 1st TR: Michael Stoger - 1997

First Ascents

Apprehension   5.8............................. Brad Beaver, Curtis Olson, Dwight Allen, Craig Malone - 1976
Arm Blaster   5.13b/c (The Ant Lobe). Michael Stoger - 2002
Arrow, The   5.8................................... John McLeod - circa 1973
N Back Drop   V6.................................... Michael Stoger - 5/02
Back Slide   5.10a/b........................... Sandy Epeldi, Dan & Georgeanne Smith - 7/96
Bad Dog   5.10b................................. Jeff Landers, Steve Young - circa 1990
N Bag of Stems   5.7   r......................... Bob Boyles, Mike Weber - mid 1970s
Barry, Barry   5.8............................... Charlie Crist, Barry DeWane - circa 1973
Basic Training   5.10a........................ Cade Lloyd, Pete Takeda, Trent Smith - c. 1983
Bat Face   5.12c   tr............................ 1st TR: Michael Stoger - 1995
Beef Curtain   5.10d........................... Tedd Thompson, Pokey Amory - 2/88
Beef Man   5.12d................................ Michael Stoger - 1997
Beta Junkie   5.10c............................ Matt Fritz, Bruce Bedell - circa 1989
Beta Sponge   5.11a........................... Steve Young - circa 1991
Big Boss Man   V5.............................. Michael Stoger - 1995
Big Crack   5.9.................................. Al Botticelli, Curtis Olson - circa 1976
N Big Roof   5.11b   tr............................. 1st TR: Bob Jahn - circa 1975
Big Times   V5................................... Todd Montgomery, Trent Smith - late 1980s
Bird Shit Man   5.12a   r....................... Michael Stoger - 1998
Black Angus   5.13a........................... Michael Stoger - 1997
Black Angus with Power   5.13b.......... Michael Stoger - 1999
Black Magic   5.9   r............................ Cade Lloyd, Pete Takeda, Trent Smith - c. 1982
Blodo Manfreak   5.11c...................... Michael Stoger - 1997
Bloody Crack   5.9.............................. Charlie Crist, Barry DeWane - circa 1973
� Bologna Pony   5.10d........................ Tedd Thompson, Rob Hart, Todd Montgomery - circa 1986
N 🎗 Bolts-n-Burger   5.8+........................... unknown
🔥 Bondi Beach   5.13a   tr..................... Steve Bullen - 1988
Bonsai   5.10c................................... Michael Stoger - 1996
� 🎣 Boogers on a Lampshade   5.12a   r.... Tedd Thompson - 1986
Boot Flake   5.10a............................. Curtis Olson - 1978
Borrowed Trouble   5.10c   tr.............. 1st TR: Todd Montgomery, Trent Smith - c. 1995
Bosom Buddies   5.10a...................... Sandy Epeldi, Sarah Brandenberger - 5/01
Boys-r-Blue   5.10b........................... Jay Aguinaga - 1997
Brand-new Secondhand   5.10b......... Isaac Madarieta, Pete Pollard - 7/02
Bretteljause   5.10a........................... Michael Stoger - 1996
Bryan's Route   5.8........................... Dan Smith, Sandy Epeldi - 11/97
BSU Fantasy   5.9.............................. Steve Fransen - 4/95
Bullworker   5.12c.............................. Michael Stoger - 1996
🔥 Burning Bush   5.10a........................ Bob Jahn - 1974
Bushwhacker   5.7.............................. Nate Marshall - 1997
Butt Start Boys, The   5.11a.............. Isaac Madarieta, P. Pollard, B. Fedigan - 8/02
Buttface   5.10b................................. Steve Young, Jeff Landers - 1990
Bwana the Mighty Met. Hunter 5.11a. Steve Fransen, Kate Cahill, Cindy Biles - 1996
Candy Ass   5.10a.............................. Sandy Epeldi, Sarah Brandenberger - 10/00
Cat Face   5.10a................................ Lee Liberty, Steve Riccio - 1995
Cat's Pajamas, The   5.10d................ Jesse "SuS" Edmundson - 7/00
Cave Left   5.9+................................. John Rozell, Curtis Olson - 1978
Cave Right   5.8................................ Curtis Olson - 1978
🎣 🎣 Chasin'-a-Snake   5.11d..................... Michael Stoger, Tedd Thompson - fall 1986
Chef Party   5.12d.............................. Michael Stoger - 1996
N Chemotherapy   5.11d   tr.................. 1st TR: Chris Parker - circa 1982
� Chicken Wings Var.   5.11c................ Tedd Thompson, Rob Hart - circa 1986

First Ascents

Chronic Load 5.11b........................... Pokey Amory, Tedd Thompson - circa 1988
Chunky Monkey 5.11b/c.................. Ted Vavricka - circa 1995; REB: Rob Welch, Steve Fransen
➤ Circuit Breaker 5.10b..................... Steve Fransen, Eric Stickland - circa 1994
Circumciser 5.10a/b......................... Sandy Epeldi, Dan Smith - 10/95
N Citizens Against Spiders 5.9............ Curtis Olson - 1976
Claptrap V4.. Tom McLeod - circa 1982
N Cleaning Lady, The 5.8..................... Frank Florence - circa 1975
Colonoscopy 5.13a/b tr.....................1st TR: Michael Stoger - 1998
Computer Girl 5.9 P1...................... Steve Fransen, Kate Cahill - 1996
Computer Girl 5.8 P2...................... Steve Fransen, Kate Cahill, J. Aguinaga - 1997
Conan 5.11b.. Michael Stoger - 1997
✐ Cool for Cats 5.11c r........................Tom McLeod - circa 1985
Copperhead 5.10a........................... Tom McLeod - circa 1978
Cotton Mouth 5.8.............................. Curtis Olson, Mike Weber - 1976
N Coup de Ville 5.8.............................. Curtis Olson, Al Botticelli, Dwight Allen - 1976
Crank Cream 5.12c...........................Tedd Thompson, Pete Takeda - circa 1988
➤ Crunchy Frogs 5.9+......................... Bruce Bedell - 1989
Crystal, The V1................................ Charlie Crist - circa 1972
Curt's Boot 5.7................................ Curtis Olson, Al Botticelli - 1975
D.O.A. 5.10a..................................... Tom McLeod - circa 1982
Daisy-Head Mayzie 5.12a.................Jesse "SuS" Edmundson - 7/02
N ✐ Dawn Patrol 5.8.............................. unknown
Day After, The 5.11d tr.....................1st TR: Tedd Thompson - circa 1986
Deep Throat 5.12c............................Michael Stoger - 1996
Defiance 5.10a................................. Curtis Olson, Brad Beaver - 1976
Deliverance 5.10a............................Tom Berge, Sandy Epeldi - circa 1992
Desperate Indulgence 5.11a............ Rob Hart, Tedd Thompson - circa 1987
Doctor Hemlock 5.10a..................... Todd Montgomery, Tedd Thompson, Steve Fransen, Almer Casile, Allison Frisbee - 1995
Dog Face 5.11a................................ Mathew Henderson, Steve Riccio - 1995
Dos Pescadores 5.10c.....................Steve Fransen, T. Hamilton, B. Whitney - 6/00
N Doug Scott Route, The 5.9+............. Doug Scott - circa 1974
➤ Drugs 5.12a/b................................. Michael Stoger, Tedd Thompson, Darius Azin - spring 1987
Drunken Sailor 5.14a....................... Michael Stoger - 1996
Dying for Dollars 5.11d tr................1st TR: Michael Stoger, Tedd Thompson - c.1986
N Eaves Drop V7................................ Michael Stoger - 1996
Ehrlichman 5.12c.............................. Michael Stoger - 1996
N El Hedor 5.10a r.............................. Michael Stoger - 1998
Energy Crisis 5.10a.........................Tom McLeod - circa 1975
N ✐ Epic for the Masses 5.7.................. unknown
✐ Excalibur 5.10a................................Tedd Thompson, Ian Smith - circa 1981
● Extrovert 5.11d tr...........................1st TR: Tom McLeod - circa 1987
➤ Fairway to Heaven 5.10b.................Sandy Epeldi, Phil Johnson, Nick Ray - 1991
N Falling Object 5.9+............................John Rozell, Mike Weber - circa 1977
N ✐ Fat Ankles 5.7.................................Charlie Crist - circa 1975
Fat Man's Misery 5.11c....................Michael Stoger - 1996
Feelin' Green 5.9.............................. Sandy Epeldi, Dan Smith, John Laughlin - 10/96
Fill the Bill 5.10b tr...........................1st TR: Todd Montgomery, Trent Smith - 1994
N Fire in the Hole V4............................ Michael Stoger - 1995
N ➤ Firefighter 5.10a...............................unknown
Fishhead Buttplug 5.10b.................. Arlo Wonacott - 1994
Flakes 5.10d (The Ant Lobe)............Michael Stoger - 2002

First Ascents

Flight 1713 5.11c.............................. Tedd Thompson, Tom McLeod - 1987
Floating on Gravel 5.10d................... Tedd Thompson - 1982
N Fly By the Seat of Your Pants V5....... Michael Stoger - 1996
Fly the Friendly Skies 5.10a.............. Cade Lloyd - circa 1984
Folley, The 5.8.................................... Curtis Olson, Dwight Allen - circa 1976
Force Dir., The V8 (The Ant Lobe)....Michael Stoger - 2002
Force, The 5.13a (The Ant Lobe)..... Michael Stoger - 2002
N Forgotten Crack 5.8......................... Mike Weber, Bob Boyles - circa 1975
Fortress Regular Route, The V0....... Tom Naylor - circa 1970
Fotzhobel 5.12c r............................. Michael Stoger - 1989
Freaky Toy Girl 5.10d...................... Sandy Epeldi, Dan & Georgeanne Smith - 7/96
Free Sample 5.9................................ Dave Cook, Jake Meissner - 10/96
French Fried 5.10a/b........................ Jay Aguinaga - 1997
French Whore 5.10c.......................... Tedd Thompson - 1997
Frosted Flake 5.10c.......................... Tedd Thompson - circa 1980
Full Bred 5.10a................................. Todd Montgomery - circa 1998
Full Tilt Boogie 5.10d....................... Steve Fransen, Cindy Biles - 1996
Funky 5.9.. Mathew Henderson, Steve Riccio - circa 1995
Furst as Sent 5.8+ r......................... Bob Allen - circa 1991
G W Loves Peanut Butter 5.9........... Sandy Epeldi, John Laughlin - 10/96
Garden, The 5.10c............................ Jeremy Johnson, Shawn Johnson - 5/97
Garnet Fever 5.11b A0.................... Sandy Epeldi - 9/95
N Genesis 3:7 5.6............................... Bob Boyles, Mike Weber - circa 1977
Girdle, The 5.9 A1............................ Curtis Olson, John Rozell, Mike Weber - 1979
N Gnarly Stump 5.9............................ Michael Stoger - 1997
⌀ God 5.13b...................................... Darius Azin - spring 1987
N Good Dog 5.9.................................. Tom McLeod - circa 1976
Good Friday 5.10a............................ Todd Montgomery, A. Casile, A. Frisbee - 1995
Goodbye Mr. Purple 5.11c............... Steve Fransen, Kate Cahill - 1996
Gravity Bath 5.10a/b........................ Nick Ray, Sandy Epeldi - 1992
Green Eggs and Ham 5.11a............. Matt Fritz - 2002
Greetings from Brownie 5.11d.......... Michael Stoger - 1997
Groveler 5.11d.................................. Steve Young, Matt Fritz - circa 1992
Gully, The 5.7................................... Frank Florence - early 1970s
☀ Hakenkruez 5.12a tr...................... 1st TR: Michael Stoger - 1986
Happy Face 5.11b............................. Mathew Henderson - 1995
Hara-Kari in a Combine 5.11b/c........ Joe Wyatt, Sam Crego - circa 1992
Heart of Darkness 5.10b.................. Ben Smith, Sandy Epeldi - 8/99
Heat Miser 5.7.................................. Kate Cahill, Steve Fransen - 1996
N ⌀ Helen's Pock Marked Face 5.8+....... unknown
Hell 5.13 A0 (The Ant Lobe)............ Michael Stoger - 2002
N Henry Barber Route 5.10d/5.11a..... Henry Barber - mid 1970s
Henry Barber's Arête 5.12d/5.13a.... Michael Stoger - 1997
Hershey Squirt 5.10c........................ Eduardo "Lalo" Rincon - 1998
N Hex Breaker 5.11c........................... Bob Jahn - 1980
High Voltage 5.10b tr...................... 1st TR: Bob Allen - circa 1991
Hilti Dust 5.11b................................ Steve Fransen, Cindy Biles - 1996
Holiday in Cambodia 5.10b.............. Steve Fransen, Kate Cahill - 1996
Horrible Human History 5.10c.......... Tedd Thompson - circa 1984
N Hot Flash 5.11b............................... Michael Stoger, Mark Motes - 11/97
Hotu Matua's Line 5.9...................... Michael Stoger, Sean Wolff - 5/02
How Now Brown Cow 5.11a............. Michael Stoger - 1997
Hufs 5.12d.. Michael Stoger - 1996
☀ I Stone 5.11c tr.............................. 1st TR: Todd Montgomery - circa 1987

182

First Ascents

In Cahoots 5.10c tr........................... 1st TR: Todd Montgomery, Trent Smith - c. 1995
In Vitro 5.10a................................... Todd Montgomery, Trent Smith - 1994
In Vivo 5.10a.................................... Todd Montgomery - circa 1997
In Your Face 5.11a/b......................... Jeff Landers - 1990
Inbred 5.10b tr................................ 1st TR: Todd Montgomery, Steve Fransen - 1995
N Industrial Age, The 5.8..................... unknown
N Introvert 5.11c tr............................ 1st TR: Dan McHale - circa 1975
Iron Man Traverse, The 5.12c........... Michael Stoger - 1993
Irreconcilable Differences 5.10a....... Sandy Epeldi, Dan Smith, John Laughlin - 10/96
It's a Peach V2................................. Michael Stoger - spring 2003
It's Not My Corner 5.11a tr.............. 1st TR: Todd Montgomery - 1980s
Jet Screamin' Hooter Queens 5.11b Matt Fritz, Steve Young - circa 1991
Jim Fall Memorial, The 5.11b........... Kip Leon Guerrero, Jim Fall - circa 1992
Joe Pro 5.10a.................................. Steve Fransen, Jay Aguinaga - 1997
Jump Chump 5.9.............................. Steve Fransen, Jay Aguinaga - 1997
Jump Start 5.11c.............................. Michael Stoger - 1996
Jungle Book 5.10a............................ Scott Urban, Robert Russell - 1995
Junkie Cosmonaut 5.12c.................. Michael Stoger - 1995; REB: Sandy Epeldi
Kaminwurtzen 5.10b.......................... Michael Stoger, Dan Smith - 1996
Kaopectate 5.12c............................. Tedd Thompson - spring 1987
King Arthur 5.10a r........................... Tedd Thompson - early 1980s
N King With a Crowbar, The 5.9........... Charlie Crist - circa 1976
N Kip to a Handstand 5.11b................. Kirk Anderson, Kip Leon Guerrero - circa 1990
N Kon-Tiki 5.12b tr.............................. 1st tr: Michael Stoger, Sean Wolff - 5/02
Layback, The 5.9+............................ Frank Florence, Mike Weber, Bob Boyles - c. '77
Lead Foot 5.9.................................. Sandy Epeldi, Nick Ray - 1990
Left Route 5.9+................................ Bob Boyles, Mike Weber - late 1970s
Leslie's Dirty Crack 5.9 r................. Richard Alva - 7/00
N Lichen Lunch 5.10c.......................... Tedd Thompson - circa 1984
Life Without Beer 5.10b.................... Sandy Epeldi, Phil Johnson - 7/95
Lightning Crack 5.8.......................... Curtis Olson - circa 1976
Lights Out 5.11a.............................. Tedd Thompson - circa 1986
Lithium Deficiency 5.11a.................. Tedd Thompson - early 1980s
N Little Nest 5.7................................. unknown
Lizard Breath 5.10a........................... Steve Fransen, Shaylin Peck - 1996
Long and Winding Road, The 5.11d.. Sandy Epeldi, John Laughlin - 8/97
Loose Tooth, The 5.7....................... Curtis Olson, Bob Boyles, Mike Weber - c. 1976
Loss of Face 5.10a........................... Steve Riccio, Mathew Henderson - 1994
Lost Arrow 5.10b............................. Tom McLeod - circa 1979
Lucky Pierre 5.9............................... Dan Smith, G. Smith, S. Epeldi, J. Laughlin - 9/95
Macabre Roof 5.10b.......................... Tom McLeod - circa 1975
Mad Cow Disease 5.13d.................. Michael Stoger - 1997
Master's Edge, The V2...................... Tom McLeod - circa 1982
Mastermind V7/8.............................. Michael Stoger - spring 2003
Matilda 5.11c.................................. Michael Stoger - 1997
Matilda's Mad Cow Disease 5.13b.... Michael Stoger - 1997
Max V 5.11b.................................... Matt Fritz - 1999
Mean Adene 5.10b/c......................... Scott Urban, Rob Russell - 12/01
Mean Chunk of Candy 5.12a............ Michael Stoger - 1996; REB: Steve Fransen
Melanie 5.9.................................... Tedd Thompson - circa 1982
Men Who Pause 5.11b...................... Tedd Thompson, Pokey Amory - 2/88
Mental Block 5.9.............................. Jeremy Johnson, Shawn Johnson - 7/97
Micro Seam 5.11d tr......................... Tom McLeod - circa 1985
Microman V3.................................... Pete Takeda - circa 1982

First Ascents

Midnight Visitor 5.10b .... Sandy Epeldi, Dan Smith - 8/95
Mike the Dog 5.10a .... Bob Mosely, Dan Smith, Mike the Dog - 1998
N Mike's Linkup V8 .... Michael Stoger - 1996
Mind Killer 5.11c .... Matt Fritz, Steve Young - circa 1993
N Minuteman 5.8 .... Curtis Olson, Al Botticelli - 1976
Misty Flip 5.10a tr .... 1st TR: Jeff Smith, Tedd Thompson - 1997
Moby's Dick 5.7 .... Bob Boyles, Mike Weber - circa 1973
Modern Mythology 5.10b .... Sandy Epeldi, John Laughlin - 11/95
Moisture Missile 5.11a .... Michael Stoger - 1986
More Than I Can Chew 5.9 .... Doyle Finch, Eduardo "Lalo" Rincon, Jay
 Aguinaga - 2001
Muchachas Borrachas 5.9 .... Steve Fransen, Jay Aguinaga - 1997
N My BackYard 5.8 .... Charlie Crist - mid 1970s
My Own Sandbox 5.13b .... Michael Stoger - 1997
My Stinky Hole 5.10c .... Dustin Buckthal, Taylor Jensen - 1998
Nash-E-Mun 5.7 .... Shah Bhatti, Dan Smith, John Laughlin - 1997
Nemesis 5.11c r .... Tom McLeod - circa 1985
Neon Leprechaun 5.10a .... Tedd Thompson, Rob Hart - circa 1985
Neon Nazi 5.10d r .... Pete Takeda - circa 1985
No Dental Records 5.11d .... Tom McLeod, Charlie Crist - circa 1990
No Name V6 .... Michael Stoger - spring 2003
No Nombre 5.10d tr .... 1st TR: Eduardo "Lalo" Rincon - 1998
N No Pro 5.10a/b r .... Michael Stoger, Mark Motes - 11/97
Nose, The 5.6 .... Curtis Olson, Dwight Allen - 1978
Nuclear Sunrise 5.12b tr .... 1st TR: Tom McLeod - circa 1988
N Nuclear Sunset 5.12a/b tr .... 1st TR: Bob John - 1980
Number Eight 5.9 .... Frank Florence - circa 1974
Number Eight Left 5.9 .... F. Florence or C. Olson or C. Crist? - mid 1970s
Number Eight Var. 5.9 .... Frank Florence - circa 1974
Number Nine 5.8 .... Charlie Crist, Barry DeWane - circa 1973
Oak Bush 5.10a .... Curtis Olson - 1978
Odyssey, The 5.9 .... Cade Lloyd, Pete Takeda - circa 1983
Oliver 5.9 .... Michael Stoger, Dan Smith - 1996
Onion Boy 5.10c .... Tedd Thompson, Todd Montgomery, Steve
 Fransen, Almer Casile, Allison Frisbee - 1995
Optimator 5.12d/5.13a .... Michael Stoger - 1997
Order from Anarchy 5.11b .... Jeremy Johnson, Shawn Johnson - 1997
Overlord 5.11d .... Matt Fritz - 5/88
N Pabst Smear 5.10b .... Tom McLeod - circa 1975
Pansy, The 5.10a .... Todd Montgomery, Steve Fransen, Allison
 Frisbee - 1995
Parking Problem 5.10d tr .... 1st TR: Steve Fransen, Jay Aguinaga, Kate
 Cahill - 1997
Peach Face, The V4 .... Michael Stoger - spring 2003
Peaches V7/8 .... Michael Stoger - spring 2003
Peachonator, The V6/7 .... Michael Stoger - spring 2003
Peanut Butter Pockets V2 .... Jeff Landers - circa 1990
Penicillin V2 .... Tedd Thompson - circa 1980
Perception vs. Reality 5.10a .... Steve Fransen, Chad Wambolt - 1994
Petty Theft 5.12a .... Tedd Thompson, Rob Hart - 3/88
Physical Graffiti 5.11a/b .... Rob Hart - circa 1987
Pictures of Lily 5.11b .... Jeff Landers - circa 1991
Pigeon Holer 5.10a .... Sandy Epeldi, John Laughlin, Dan Smith - 10/96
Pigger Memorial Slab V5 .... Tedd Thompson - circa 1986

184

Pin Scars 5.12d tr............................1st TR: Tom McLeod - circa 1988
N Pink Panther, The 5.9.......................Mike Weber, John Rozell - circa 1978
Piss and Vinegar 5.9.........................Shawn Johnson, Jeremy Johnson - 5/97
⌘ Pizza Face 5.11b/c...........................Kimber Almond, Janice Bassick, B. Bedell - 1989
Plastic Yuppie Cookie Cutter 5.10a...Sandy Epeldi - 5/95
N Pocket Fisherman 5.11c tr.............. Jeff Landers - circa 1991
N Pocket Pool 5.11b tr........................ Jeff Landers - circa 1991
Poodle Boy 5.10a............................Todd Montgomery, Trent Smith - 1994
Popsicle Stand Var. 5.11c tr.............1st TR: Todd Montgomery, Trent Smith - 1994
Power Failure 5.10a......................... Tom McLeod - circa 1975
Power Ranger 5.12c........................ Michael Stoger - 1994
Power Trip V9................................. Michael Stoger - 1998
N Prominent Crack 5.9....................... Bob Jahn - circa 1975
N ⚭ Promiscuity Crack 5.10b..................unknown
Propeller 5.11d............................. Tedd Thompson - circa 1980
N ⚭ Psalm 23 Left 5.10a......................Mike Weber, Bob Boyles - circa 1977
Psalm 23 Right 5.10c...................... Grant Walker - circa 1988
Psalm 55 5.10a............................. Grant Walker - circa 1988
Public Service 5.10b........................ Jeff Smith - 1997
Puffer, The 5.9................................. Steve Fransen, Kate Cahill - 1996
Quarry Crack 5.11b tr.................... 1st TR: Tom McLeod - circa 1985
Quarry Man, The 5.12d.................... Michael Stoger - 1997
Rainbow Warrior 5.12a/b................. Sandy Epeldi, Sarah Brandenberger - 10/00
Raisin the Titanic 5.10b................... Tedd Thompson - early 1980s
Ramp, The 5.6................................ Mike Weber, Bob Boyles - circa 1972
Red Bull 5.12b................................Michael Stoger - 1996
Red Sonja 5.11c............................. Michael Stoger - 1997
Red Toenails 5.9+........................... Craig Prather - circa 1989
Red Wall V6.................................. Michael Stoger - 1997
N Reducer 5.11c................................Michael Stoger - 1996
Remnant, The 5.11c........................ Todd Montgomery, Trent Smith - 1994
Ren and Stemmy 5.11a................... Steve Young, Matt Fritz - circa 1994
⚭ Resignation 5.11a............................ Michael Stoger - 1996
N ⌘ Rhus Radicans 5.8+........................unknown
N Right of Arête 5.11d tr..................... 1st TR: Tom McLeod - circa 1985
N Rigid Digits 5.10c............................Tom McLeod - circa 1981
Road Kill 5.12a/b............................ Tom McLeod, Charlie Crist - circa 1990
Road Runner 5.12c tr.................... 1st TR: Michael Stoger, Tedd Thompson - 1986
N Roadside Boulder Problem V0..........John Platt - circa 1973
Robinson Crusoe's Workout 5.13a...Michael Stoger, Sean Wolff - 5/02
⚭ ⚲ Rock Hudson 5.11a........................Cade Lloyd - circa 1983
Rodeo Flips 5.10a............................Jeff Smith, Tedd Thompson - 1997
Rosy Palms 5.11c............................Sandy Epeldi - 6/01
Row Your Boat 5.10a........................Steve Fransen, Cindy Biles - 6/00
S Crack 5.9................................... Mike Weber, Bob Boyles - late 1970s
Safe Sex Subaru 5.10a..................... Tedd Thompson, Rob Hart - circa 1986
⚭ Safety Dance 5.10b.........................Cade Lloyd - circa 1983
⌘ Salad Shooter 5.11a...................... Sandy Epeldi, Brian Jaszkowiak - 10/97
Salad Shooter Dir. 5.11d.................. Sandy Epeldi, Brian Fedigan - 5/01
Saturn 5.12c..................................Michael Stoger - 1995; REB: Morgan Waldorf
Saturn Dir. 5.13a............................ Michael Stoger - 10/02
Saving Face 5.9+............................Steve Riccio - 1994
Scapula 5.8................................... Curtis Olson - 1975
N Scoop All the Way, The 5.12a tr....... 1st TR: Bob Jahn - circa 1977

First Ascents

N ⌒ Scream, The 5.10b........................... unknown
Seven Moai, The 5.10d.....................Michael Stoger, Sean Wolff - 5/02
Shades of Gray 5.10b..................... Sandy Epeldi, Ben Smith - 8/99
N Shelf Life 5.10b................................ Michael Stoger - 1998
Shelf, The V5.................................... Michael Stoger - spring 2003
Shimmey 5.7.....................................Curtis Olson, Dwight Allen - fall 1976
Shish KeBOB V6.............................. Kip Leon Guerrero - circa 1993
Shit on Flies 5.10d tr........................1st TR: Todd Montgomery, Trent Smith - 1994
N Short but Sweet 5.11c..................... Tom McLeod, Charlie Crist - circa 1990
Simon Says 5.11b tr........................1st TR: Todd Montgomery, Trent Smith - 1980s
Simple Physics 5.10a..................... Steve Fransen - 1995
N Sixty-Three 5.8................................Mike Weber, Bob Boyles - circa 1977
N Slip Fault V4.................................... Michael Stoger - 5/02
Slot Traverse, The 5.12....................Michael Stoger - spring 2003
Smelly Dark Hole 5.13a....................Michael Stoger - 12/02
Snake Eyes 5.8................................ Todd Montgomery, Remington Turner - 1997
Snapper 5.7.....................................Sandy Epeldi, John Laughlin - 7/98
Snow Miser 5.10b.............................Mike Rishel - 9/00
Soft Parade 5.12a............................ Matt Fritz, Steve Young, Bruce Bedell - c. 1990
Something of Nothing 5.12c tr.......... 1st TR: Tom McLeod - circa 1988
Sooner or Later 5.12c.......................Michael Stoger - 1998
N Spasm 5.8.. Frank Florence - circa 1975
Spear, The 5.10c.............................. Dan McHale, Charlie Crist - circa 1974
Specialist, The 5.11b.......................Michael Stoger - 1996
Sperm Whale 5.11b...........................Matt Fritz, Steve Young, Bruce Bedell - c. 1990
Spice of Life Dir., The 5.11b.............. Smith Kennedy, Steve Fransen - 6/00
Spiny Trouble 5.10b........................... Steve Fransen, Jay Aguinaga - 1997
Spunky 5.9+ tr................................ 1st TR: Steve Riccio, Mathew Henderson - c. '95
N Squatter's Right V6........................... Michael Stoger - 5/02
Standard, The 5.6............................ Mike Weber, Bob Boyles - fall 1972
Standard Direct, The 5.7................. Mike Weber, Bob Boyles - circa 1975
Standard Right, The 5.8....................Bob Boyles, Mike Weber - circa 1975
Star, The V4 (Valley of the Trolls)...... Tom McLeod - circa 1980
Steal Your Face 5.11b....................... Tom McLeod - 1990
Steel Monkey 5.13b/c....................... Michael Stoger - 1996
Steel Monkey/ Wupit Combo 5.13a...Michael Stoger - 1999
Steep Disorder 5.10c........................ Sandy Epeldi, Dan Smith, John Laughlin - 10/95
Stem Corner 5.12a tr....................... 1st TR: Tom McLeod - circa 1982
Stemulus 5.11d................................ Matt Fritz, Steve Young - circa 1989
N Stemulus Crack 5.9.........................Bob Boyles, Curt Olson - circa 1981
Stepping Razor 5.11c.......................Isaac Madarieta, Pete Pollard, S. Epeldi - 7/02
Sting Var., The 5.13a........................ Michael Stoger, Tonja Stoger - 1995
Sting, The 5.12d................................ Tony Yaniro, Tedd Thompson - 3/88
N Stoger's Traverse V7....................... Michael Stoger - 1994
⌒ Stone Tools 5.10b............................. John Laughlin, Sandy Epeldi - 1995
N Stretch Armstrong 5.11d tr.............. 1st TR: Jeff Landers - early 1990s
N Sudden Meltdown V4....................... Michael Stoger - 1994
Sugar Baby 5.11a.............................Michael Stoger - 1997
Super Cacho 5.13d/5.14a................ Michael Stoger - 1999
Super Crack V2................................ Bob Jahn - circa 1979
Super Mastermind 5.14-.................. Michael Stoger - spring 2003
Superman Traverse, The V6............. Michael Stoger - 1993
N Surf's Up 5.9+.................................unknown - circa 1974
Sweat Drenched Flannel 5.10c.........Steve Fransen, Shaylin Peck - 1996

Sweat Engine 5.10d...........................Steve Fransen, Jacob Sack - 4/95
Sweet Adene 5.8...........................Corbin Olsen, Steve Fransen - circa 1994
N Sweet and Sour 5.8...........................Curtis Olson - 1976
Sweet Thing 5.9...............................Jay Aguinaga - 1997
Swimmin' in Ignorance 5.10a.............Steve Fransen, Kate Cahill - 1996
T.V.O.D. 5.12b.............................Tedd Thompson, Michael Stoger - fall 1986
N Temple, The 5.10a...........................Curtis Olson, Al Botticelli - circa 1978
Terminal Hypocrisy 5.10b.................Steve Fransen, E. Stickland, E. Hansen - 1994
Thanks for the Mammaries 5.11a.....Doug Colwell, Steve Young - circa 1991
Thin line 5.10d r............................. Tom McLeod - circa 1977
Three Amigos 5.12a tr....................1st TR: Dusty Pena, Grant Walker, Nikos Sawyer - 2/88
Throb, The 5.11a...........................Tedd Thompson - circa 1979
Thursday Knights 5.10b...................Walter Fields, Taylor Jensen - 1999
Tidy Up 5.10a.................................Todd Montgomery, Trent Smith - 1994
Tin Man 5.11b/c.............................Matt Fritz, Steve Young, Bruce Bedell - c. 1990
Toddler 5.6..Jay Aguinaga, Andrea Loveland, "Augi" Aguinaga - 1998
N Tom Cat 5.10d r.............................. Tom McLeod, Doug Colwell - circa 1985
N Tom's Corner V3.............................. Tom McLeod - circa 1984
N Tony's Arête 5.12b tr........................1st TR: Tony Yaniro - circa 1987
Too Easy 5.11d.................................Michael Stoger - 1997
Tool Boys 5.10b..............................Brian Fedigan, S. Epeldi, I. Madarieta - 8/02
Traverse of the Dogs 5.11d............. Michael Stoger - 1997
N Trimmed Bush, The 5.10a.............Curtis Olson, Craig Malone - 1978
N Tweak of the Devil V6.............................. Michael Stoger - 1995
Twinkle Toes 5.10b...........................Kimber Almond, Sandy Epeldi - 1989
Two Finger Pocket V3......................Michael Stoger - 1993
Ugly Duckling 5.10a..........................Jay Aguinaga, Donnell Aguinaga - 1998
N Under the Table V6............................Michael Stoger - 1994
Undercling to Pocket V5...................Michael Stoger - 1993
Unknown Leon 5.11a...................... Rob Hart, Tedd Thompson - circa 1988
Urge to Purge 5.9............................John Laughlin, Sandy Epeldi - 10/96
Vapor Lock 5.12a.............................Tedd Thompson, Michael Stoger - 1989
Velcro Fly 5.10b..............................Matt Fritz - circa 1984
Vertical Slur 5.12c tr.........................1st TR: Tedd Thompson - circa 1986
Virgin, The 5.11b.............................Tedd Thompson - circa 1982
N Wailing Offwidth 5.8.........................Mike Weber, Bob Boyles - circa 1977
Warm Up V1....................................Michael Stoger - spring 2003
Watergate 5.12c...............................Michael Stoger - 1996
Weenie Roast 5.10c..........................Steve Young, Bruce Bedell - circa 1989
West Wall Won, 5.9 r...................... Curtis Olson, Vernon Kindred - circa 1980
Whaleback Crack 5.7.......................Pete Takeda - early 1980s
Whimper 5.9....................................Steve Fransen, T. Montgomery, A. Frisbee - 1995
N White Wash 5.9...............................Charlie Crist, Barry DeWane - circa 1974
Whole Lotta Nothing 5.12b tr........... 1st TR: Tom McLeod - circa 1988
Wimp Roof 5.11c..............................Tom McLeod, Tedd Thompson, Pete Takeda - circa 1983
Win, Lose or Draw 5.10c..................Jay Aguinaga - 1997
Wire Brush Haircut 5.12a................Tom McLeod - circa 1985
Woolly Footed Vixen 5.10a.............. Rob Hart - circa 1986
Wounded Knee 5.8+ r......................Bob Boyles, Frank Florence - circa 1975
Wupit 5.12c.......................................Michael Stoger, Mark Motes - 1998
Your Face or Mine 5.11c..................Bruce Bedell, Doug Brown - 1990

Gear Routes

5.5
- ❑ Chimney
- ❑ Staircase
- ❑ Tree Route, The

5.6
- ❑ Carnaval
- ❑ Easy Crack
- ❑ Easy Cracks
- ❑ First Lead
- ❑ Gargling Vinegar
- ❑ Genesis 3:7
- ❑ Nose, The
- ❑ Pioneer Crack
- ❑ Ramp, The
- ❑ Stacked
- ❑ Standard, The

5.7
- ❑ 3 guys and 3 Cracks #3
- ❑ A Dirt Bag and Lichen It
- ❑ Arachnophobia
- ❑ Bag of Stems
- ❑ Burgermeister Meisterberger
- ❑ Buster Bronco
- ❑ Center Route, The
- ❑ Curt's Boot
- ❑ Eyeless In Gaza
- ❑ Gully, The
- ❑ Jenga
- ❑ Lancelot
- ❑ Left Grunge Tower, The
- ❑ Loaded Gun
- ❑ Loose Tooth
- ❑ Moby's Dick
- ❑ Old Toll Route, The
- ❑ Raptor's Revenge
- ❑ Right Grunge Tower, The
- ❑ Rotten Nest
- ❑ School Daze
- ❑ Shimmey
- ❑ Standard Direct, The
- ❑ Steve's Offwidth
- ❑ Sugar Magnolia
- ❑ Wagon Rut, The
- ❑ Whaleback Crack

5.8
- ❑ 3 Guys and 3 Cracks #2
- ❑ 409
- ❑ Apprehension
- ❑ Arrow, The
- ❑ Aunt Fannie
- ❑ Barry, Barry
- ❑ Boulder Holder
- ❑ Cave Right
- ❑ Cleaning Lady, The
- ❑ Cochise Crack
- ❑ Constant Current
- ❑ Cotton Mouth
- ❑ Coupe de Ville
- ❑ Deuteronomy 23:13
- ❑ Dirty Luck
- ❑ Easy Thirteen
- ❑ Feng Shui
- ❑ Folley, The
- ❑ Forgotten Crack
- ❑ Generic Crack
- ❑ Layback Crack
- ❑ Lightning Crack
- ❑ Little Boots
- ❑ Loaded Question
- ❑ Minuteman
- ❑ My Backyard
- ❑ Nikita
- ❑ Number Nine
- ❑ Nut 'n a Sling
- ❑ Obvious Crack
- ❑ Orientationally Confused
- ❑ Populace Offwidth
- ❑ Potato Flake
- ❑ Scapula
- ❑ Short Crack
- ❑ Sixty-Three
- ❑ Snake Corner
- ❑ Spasm
- ❑ Squirt Gun
- ❑ Standard Right, The
- ❑ Stems & Jammies
- ❑ Sweet and Sour
- ❑ Two Studs
- ❑ Up in Smoke
- ❑ Wailing Offwidth
- ❑ Wise One, The

5.8+
- ❑ Big Fat Crack
- ❑ Father, The
- ❑ Flying Circus, The
- ❑ Furst as Sent
- ❑ Jen's Dilemma
- ❑ Man Eater
- ❑ Mathew's Offwidth
- ❑ Mourning Star
- ❑ Wabbit Hunta
- ❑ Wounded Knee

5.9
- ❑ Almond Roof
- ❑ Beavis
- ❑ Big Crack
- ❑ Big Head Ed
- ❑ Black Magic

Gear Routes

- ❏ Bloody Crack
- ❏ Citizens Against Spiders
- ❏ Divine Intervention
- ❏ Edge and Stem
- ❏ Flammable Idaho
- ❏ Funky
- ❏ G W Loves Peanut Butter
- ❏ Gnarly Stump
- ❏ Good Dog
- ❏ Hotu Matua's Line
- ❏ Jim Fall Memorial Var., The
- ❏ Leslie's Dirty Crack
- ❏ Liberty Crack
- ❏ Lunch Ledge
- ❏ Melanie
- ❏ Mental Block
- ❏ Neophyte flight
- ❏ Number Eight Left
- ❏ Number Eight Var.
- ❏ Odyssey, The
- ❏ Ohm's Law
- ❏ Pink Panther, The
- ❏ Piss and Vinegar
- ❏ Prominent Crack
- ❏ Rectal Cranial Insertion
- ❏ Roanne's Way
- ❏ S Crack
- ❏ Shake Smear
- ❏ Speed Queen
- ❏ Stemulus Crack
- ❏ Temporary Insanity
- ❏ West Wall Won

5.9+

- ❏ Basalt Somersault
- ❏ Cave Left
- ❏ Doug Scott Route, The
- ❏ Falling Object
- ❏ Flotsam
- ❏ Helios
- ❏ Layback, The
- ❏ Left Route
- ❏ Saving Face
- ❏ Surf's Up
- ❏ Whitehead Crack

5.10a

- ❏ 3 Guys and 3 Cracks #1
- ❏ Alcohol Poisoning
- ❏ Basic Training
- ❏ Boot Flake
- ❏ Bretteljause
- ❏ Copperhead
- ❏ D.O.A.
- ❏ Defiance
- ❏ Deliverance

- ❏ Disco Crack
- ❏ Energy Crisis
- ❏ Fly the Friendly Skies
- ❏ Guano Corner
- ❏ Irreconcilable Differences
- ❏ Joe Pro
- ❏ Jungle Book
- ❏ King Arthur
- ❏ Mammon
- ❏ Married Man
- ❏ Oak Bush
- ❏ Plastic Yuppie Cookie Cutter, The
- ❏ Power Failure
- ❏ Safe Sex Subaru
- ❏ Temple, The
- ❏ Thunder Face
- ❏ Trimmed Bush, The
- ❏ Woolly Footed Vixen

5.10b

- ❏ Bird Roof
- ❏ Macabre Roof
- ❏ No Pro
- ❏ Raisin the Titanic
- ❏ Snow Miser
- ❏ Velcro Fly

5.10c

- ❏ Frosted Flake
- ❏ Garden, The
- ❏ Horrible Human History
- ❏ Rigid Digits
- ❏ Spear, The

5.10d

- ❏ Floating on Gravel
- ❏ Generic Crack Var.
- ❏ Neon Nazi
- ❏ Seven Moai, The
- ❏ Thin Line
- ❏ Tom Cat

5.10d/5.11a

- ❏ Henry Barber Route, The

5.11a

- ❏ Lithium Deficiency

5.11b

- ❏ Conan
- ❏ Jim Fall Memorial, The
- ❏ Superman Crack

5.11c

- ❏ Cool for Cats
- ❏ Hex Breaker
- ❏ Nemesis
- ❏ Rosy Palms

5.13a

- ❏ Robinson Crusoe's Workout Crack

Sport Routes

5.6
❏ Toddler

5.7
❏ Bushwhacker
❏ Epic for the Masses
❏ Fat Ankles
❏ Heat Miser
❏ Little Nest
❏ Nash-E-Mun
❏ Snapper

5.8
❏ Almer Casile Memorial Buttress
❏ Bryan's Route
❏ Computer Girl Pitch #2
❏ Dawn Patrol
❏ Industrial Age, The
❏ Red Toenails Var.
❏ Snake Eyes
❏ Sweet Adene

5.8+
❏ Bolts-n-Burger

5.9
❏ After Midnight
❏ Ajax
❏ BSU Fantasy
❏ Computer Girl Pitch #1
❏ Excalibur
❏ In Vivo
❏ Jump Chump
❏ King With a Crowbar, The
❏ Lucky Pierre
❏ More Than I Can Chew
❏ Muchachas Borrachas
❏ Number Eight
❏ Puffer, The
❏ Sweet Thing
❏ Whimper
❏ White Wash

5.9+
❏ Crunchy Frogs
❏ Red Toenails

5.10a
❏ All the Way Home
❏ Candy Ass
❏ Doctor Hemlock
❏ Full Bred
❏ Good Friday
❏ In Vitro
❏ Lizard Breath
❏ Loss of Face
❏ Neon Leprechaun
❏ Pansy, The
❏ Perception vs. Reality
❏ Poodle Boy

❏ Psalm 23 Left
❏ Psalm 55
❏ Rodeo Flips
❏ Row Your Boat
❏ Simple Physics
❏ Tidy Up
❏ Ugly Duckling

5.10a/b
❏ Back Slide
❏ Circumciser
❏ French Fried
❏ Gravity Bath

5.10b
❏ Ambition is Critical
❏ Bad Dog
❏ Boys-r-Blue
❏ Brand-new Secondhand
❏ Buttface
❏ Circuit Breaker
❏ Fairway to Heaven
❏ Fishhead Buttplug
❏ Heart of Darkness
❏ Holiday in Cambodia
❏ Kaminwurtzen
❏ Life Without Beer
❏ Lost Arrow
❏ Midnight Visitor
❏ Modern Mythology
❏ Mystery Route
❏ Pabst Smear
❏ Promiscuity Crack
❏ Public Service
❏ Safety Dance
❏ Shades of Gray
❏ Shelf Life
❏ Spice of Life, The
❏ Spiny Trouble
❏ Stone Tools
❏ Terminal Hypocrisy
❏ Thursday Knights
❏ Tool Boys

5.10b/c
❏ Mean Adene

5.10c
❏ Allison Wonderland
❏ Angry Bunnies
❏ Beta Junkie
❏ Dos Pescadores
❏ French Whore
❏ Hershey Squirt
❏ Lichen Lunch
❏ My Stinky Hole
❏ Onion Boy
❏ Psalm 23 Right

Sport Routes

- Sweat Drenched Flannel
- Win, Lose or Draw

5.10d

- Beef Curtain
- Bologna Pony
- Cat's Pajamas, The
- Freaky Toy Girl
- Full Tilt Boogie
- Sweat Engine
- Throb, The
- Thursday Knights Arête

5.11a

- Beta Sponge
- Butt Start Boys, The
- Bwana the Mighty Metolius Hunter
- Dog Face
- Green Eggs and Ham
- How Now Brown Cow
- Lights Out
- Public Service Dir.
- Ren & Stemmy
- Rock Hudson
- Salad Shooter
- Sugar Baby
- Thanks for the Mammaries
- Unknown Leon

5.11a/b

- In Your Face
- Physical Graffiti

5.11b

- Chronic Load
- Garnet Fever
- Happy Face
- Hilti Dust
- Jet Screamin' Hooter Queens
- Kip to a Handstand
- Max V
- Men Who Pause
- Pictures of Lily
- Specialist, The
- Sperm Whale
- Spice of Life Dir., The
- Steal Your Face
- Virgin, The
- Wire Brush Haircut Var.

5.11b/c

- Chunky Monkey
- Pizza Face
- Tin Man
- Win, Lose or Draw Dir. (Right)

5.11c

- Blodo Manfreak
- Fat Man's Misery
- Goodbye Mr. Purple

- Jump Start
- Matilda
- Mind Killer
- Red Sonja
- Reducer
- Remnant, The
- Stepping Razor
- Sweat Engine Dir.
- Wimp Roof
- Your Face or Mine

5.11c/d

- Another Face in the Crowd

5.11d

- Chasin'-a-Snake
- Greetings from Brownie
- Groveler
- Long and Winding Road, The
- Overlord
- Salad Shooter Dir.
- Stemulus
- Too Easy
- Traverse of the Dogs
- Win, Lose or Draw Dir. (Left)

5.12a

- Bologna Pony Var.
- Daisy-Head Mayzie
- Mean Chunk of Candy
- Men Who Pause Var.
- Petty Theft
- Soft Parade
- Vapor Lock
- Wire Brush Haircut

5.12a/b

- Drugs
- Rainbow Warrior
- Road Kill

5.12b

- Red Bull
- T.V.O.D.

5.12c

- Bullworker
- Crank Cream
- Deep Throat
- Ehrlichman
- Fotzhobel
- Junkie Cosmonaut
- Power Ranger
- Red Sonja Dir.
- Saturn
- Sooner or Later
- Watergate
- Wupit

5.12d

- Aid Roof, The

Sport & Mixed Routes

- ❏ Beef Man
- ❏ Chef Party
- ❏ Hufs
- ❏ Quarry Man, The

5.12d/5.13a
- ❏ Henry Barber's Arête
- ❏ Optimator

5.13a
- ❏ Black Angus
- ❏ Saturn Dir.
- ❏ Steel Monkey/ Wupit Combination
- ❏ Watergate Dir.

5.13b
- ❏ Black Angus with Power
- ❏ God
- ❏ Matilda's Mad Cow Disease
- ❏ My Own Sandbox

5.13b/c
- ❏ Steel Monkey

5.13d
- ❏ Mad Cow Disease

5.13d/5.14a
- ❏ Super Cacho

5.14a
- ❏ Drunken Sailor

MIXED ROUTES - gear and bolts

5.8
- ❏ Mood Swing

5.8+
- ❏ Helen's Pock Marked Face
- ❏ Rhus Radicans

5.9
- ❏ Feelin' Green
- ❏ Free Sample
- ❏ Lead Foot
- ❏ Oliver
- ❏ Urge to Purge

5.10a
- ❏ Bosom Buddies
- ❏ Cat Face
- ❏ El Hedor
- ❏ Firefighter
- ❏ Mike the Dog
- ❏ Pigeon Holer
- ❏ Sweaty Crack
- ❏ Swimmin' in Ignorance

5.10b
- ❏ Scream, The
- ❏ Twinkle Toes

5.10c
- ❏ Bonsai
- ❏ Steep Disorder
- ❏ Weenie Roast

5.11a
- ❏ Desperate Indulgence
- ❏ Resignation

5.11b
- ❏ Hot Flash
- ❏ Order from Anarchy

5.11b/c
- ❏ Hara-Kari In a Combine

5.11c
- ❏ Chicken Wings Var.
- ❏ Flight 1713
- ❏ Short but Sweet

5.11d
- ❏ No Dental Records

5.12a
- ❏ Bird Shit Man
- ❏ Boogers on a Lampshade

5.12c
- ❏ Kaopectate

5.12d
- ❏ Sting, The

5.13a
- ❏ Sting Var., The

Toprope Climbs

5.6 tr
- ❑ Bee Block, The

5.7 tr
- ❑ Turtle Rock Corner

5.9 tr
- ❑ Buffalo Slab Right
- ❑ Life Sentence
- ❑ Owl Corner
- ❑ Skinny Flake
- ❑ Watts Up?

5.9+ tr
- ❑ Dihedral
- ❑ Spunky

5.10a tr
- ❑ Buffalo Slab Left
- ❑ Dirt Corner
- ❑ Headlights in the Fog
- ❑ Kowallis and Richards Hardware Bin
- ❑ Misty Flip
- ❑ No Name
- ❑ Rotten Corner

5.10b tr
- ❑ Borrowed Shoes
- ❑ Fill the Bill
- ❑ High Voltage
- ❑ In Between
- ❑ Inbred
- ❑ Never Named
- ❑ Swallow

5.10c tr
- ❑ Abandoned Project
- ❑ Bat Crack Direct
- ❑ Bat Lunge
- ❑ Borrowed Trouble
- ❑ In Cahoots
- ❑ Matt's Crack

5.10d tr
- ❑ Dolly
- ❑ Hobnob
- ❑ No Nombre
- ❑ Parking Problem
- ❑ Riccio's Face
- ❑ Shit on Flies
- ❑ Unclaimed

5.11a tr
- ❑ Abandoned Project Var.
- ❑ Balloon Party
- ❑ It's Not My Corner
- ❑ Misfire
- ❑ Moisture Missile
- ❑ Tippy Toe
- ❑ What Crack?

5.11b tr
- ❑ Big Roof
- ❑ Buffalo Arête
- ❑ Life Sentence Top Out
- ❑ Pocket Pool
- ❑ Pure Energy
- ❑ Quarry Crack
- ❑ Simon Says
- ❑ Sugar Daddy

5.11c tr
- ❑ Pocket Fisherman
- ❑ Popsicle Stand Var.
- ❑ Revelations 13:1

5.11d tr
- ❑ Chemotherapy
- ❑ Day After, The
- ❑ Dying for Dollars
- ❑ Micro Seam
- ❑ Propeller
- ❑ Right of Arête
- ❑ Shredder
- ❑ Stretch Armstrong

5.12a tr
- ❑ Buffalo Crack
- ❑ Scoop All the Way, The
- ❑ Stem Corner
- ❑ Three Amigos

5.12a/b tr
- ❑ Nuclear Sunset

5.12b tr
- ❑ Another Stoger Route
- ❑ Kon-Tiki
- ❑ Nuclear Sunrise
- ❑ Whole Lotta Nothing

5.12c tr
- ❑ Bat Face
- ❑ Road Runner
- ❑ Something of Nothing

5.12d tr
- ❑ Buffalo Crack Dir.
- ❑ Pin Scars

5.13a/b tr
- ❑ Colonoscopy

Boulder Problems

VB

- Balance Ledge Traverse
- Blast Hole
- Buckets
- C & L Route
- California Flake Remains
- Friction Slab
- Humdrum
- Junior Achievement
- Laid Back
- Mini Crack
- Pit Fall
- Popeye
- Santa's Secret
- Slab Left
- Slap
- Table Boulder Right Corner
- Tubular
- Wayback Layback

V0-

- Bob's Nose
- Bobby's Traverse
- Boulder Crack
- Crumbling Corner
- Dirt Bag Direct
- Hunchback Layback
- Idiot Proof Traverse
- Mickey Mantel
- Poison Ivy Slab
- Slab Right

V0

- Bat Crack
- Behind the Boss
- Bloody Knuckles
- Bomb Bay
- Drill Crack
- Edging Skills
- Electric Cross Direct
- Falling Down the Mountain
- Fortress Regular Route, The
- Green-eyed Bugs
- Kobe's Forehead
- Mantel and Pop
- Mushroom, The
- Night Moves
- Nova
- Peanut Butter Left Arête
- Peanut Butter Right Arête
- Right Crack
- Roadside Boulder Problem
- Scoop, The
- Smoke Me Straight Up
- Smoke Me Traverse
- Table Boulder Lunge

- Whole Ordeal, The
- Zimbo

V0+

- Below the Roof Traverse
- Corner to Pocket Traverse
- Fortress Right Corner, The
- Great Day for Up!
- Headstone Crack
- Heel Hook
- Left Hand Start
- Nick's Problem
- Pop Tart
- Popeye Direct
- Pullover
- Sleeping Dog
- Super Boy

V1

- Bob Down Under
- Bob the Seal
- Crystal, The
- Electric Cross Traverse
- Gastons
- Lois
- Naked Edge, The
- Night Moves Overhang
- Night Moves Traverse
- Offwidth Boulder Problem
- Psycho Braille
- Swing Out Sister
- Warm Up

V2

- Comfortably Numb
- Crackerjack
- Cutting Edge Traverse, The
- DiscomBOBulator
- Drilled Pockets
- Dyno For Dollars
- Fortress Edge, The
- Fortress Lunge, The
- Hook Left
- Hop on Pop
- It's a Peach
- Master's Edge, The
- Peanut Butter Pockets
- Penicillin
- Right Hand Start
- Short Corner
- Super Crack
- Super Nova
- Sweaty Peach, The

V3

- Behind the Bush
- Bob's Lower Lip
- Ceiling Crack

Boulder Problems

- ❏ Crackerjack Without the Prize
- ❏ Grinch, The
- ❏ Kryptonite Hangover
- ❏ Microman
- ❏ Mortal Cling
- ❏ Nice Peace
- ❏ Sharp Arête
- ❏ Shpofol
- ❏ Sit Down and Smoke Me
- ❏ Tom's Corner
- ❏ Two Finger Pocket

V4
- ❏ Bob Down Under Traverse
- ❏ Car Body Traverse, The
- ❏ Chiseled Traverse
- ❏ Claptrap
- ❏ Crystal Butt Start, The
- ❏ Drawing a Blank
- ❏ Fire in the Hole
- ❏ Going Platinum
- ❏ Learning to Fly
- ❏ Peach Face, The
- ❏ Peaches and Cream
- ❏ Slip Fault
- ❏ Sudden Meltdown

V5
- ❏ Big Boss Man
- ❏ Big Times
- ❏ Fly By the Seat of Your Pants
- ❏ Fortress Traverse, The
- ❏ Pigger Memorial Slab
- ❏ Shelf, The
- ❏ Slot Traverse, The
- ❏ Superman in Reverse
- ❏ Undercling to Pocket

V6
- ❏ Back Drop
- ❏ Highway Face Traverse, The
- ❏ Iron Man Traverse, The
- ❏ No Name
- ❏ Red Wall
- ❏ Shish KeBOB
- ❏ Squatter's Right
- ❏ Superman Traverse
- ❏ Tweak of the Devil
- ❏ Under the Table

V6/V7
- ❏ Peachonator, The

V7
- ❏ Eaves Drop
- ❏ Smelly Dark Hole
- ❏ Stoger's Traverse
- ❏ Tunnel Traverse

V7/V8
- ❏ Mastermind
- ❏ Peaches

V8
- ❏ Mike's Linkup

V9
- ❏ Power Trip

V10
- ❏ Super Mastermind

Index

Index

Index

Index

Index

Index

Index

Notes

Directory
of local shops,
services and
products

The Boise Climbers Alliance

The Boise Climbers Alliance is a non-profit organization dedicated to advocating for climbers on issues regarding access, impact, and other matters, and promoting low-impact, environmentally sensitive climbing. The alliance came together in 1999 specifically to address concerns about the impact of rock climbing on nesting raptors—golden eagles and prairie falcons—at the Black Cliffs. In November 1999, the BCA announced the release of a plan intended to accomplish just that, put together in conjunction with the Idaho Department of Fish and Game.

Under the plan, the BCA posts signs in February at specific areas of the Black Cliffs where eagles and falcons have been known to nest; the signs ask climbers to avoid climbing in the immediate vicinity. Raptors will establish their nest sites between mid-winter and early spring. By April, IDFG and the BCA identify actual nest sites at the Black Cliffs, and remove signs from areas where there are no nests. Then the BCA uses local media, gear shops, and climbing gyms to spread the word to the climbing community, asking climbers to voluntarily avoid routes near established nests.

Pivotal to the plan's success is the willingness of climbers to respect seasonal, voluntary closures of critical climbing routes. These closures affect a very small percentage of routes at the cliffs, and are voluntary; the BCA carries no enforcement authority. But without the cooperation of climbers in this plan, we fear we face the possibility of future regulatory actions by land managers to protect the raptors.

Michael Lanza, BCA President
mlanza@velocitus.net
433-8652

ACCESS: It's every climber's concern

The Access Fund, a national, non-profit climbers organization, works to keep climbing areas open and to conserve the climbing environment. Need help with closures? land acquisition? legal or land management issues? funding for trails and other projects? starting a local climbers' group? CALL US!

Climbers can help preserve access by being committed to leaving the environment in its natural state. Here are some simple guidelines:

•**ASPIRE TO CLIMB WITHOUT LEAVING A TRACE,** especially in environmentally sensitive areas like caves. Chalk can be a significant impact on dark and porous rock—don't use it around historic rock art. Pick up litter, and leave trees and plants intact.

•**DISPOSE OF HUMAN WASTE PROPERLY** Use toilets whenever possible. If toilets are not available, dig a "cat hole" at least six inches deep and 200 feet from any water, trails, campsites, or the base of climbs. *Always pack out toilet paper.* On big wall routes, use a "poop tube" and carry waste up and off with you (the old "bag toss" is now illegal in many areas).

•**USE EXISTING TRAILS** Cutting switchbacks causes erosion. When walking off-trail, tread lightly, especially in the desert where cryptogamic soils (usually a dark crust) take thousands of years to form and are easily damaged. Be aware that "rimecologies" (the clifftop) are often highly sensitive to disturbance.

•**BE DISCRETE WITH FIXED ANCHORS** *Bolts are controversial and are not a convenience—don't place them unless they are really necessary.* Camouflage all anchors. Remove unsightly slings from rappel stations (better to use steel chain or welded cold shuts). Bolts sometimes can be used proactively to protect fragile resources—consult with your local land manager.

•**RESPECT THE RULES** and speak up when other climbers don't. Expect restrictions in designated wilderness areas, rock art sites, caves, and to protect wildlife, especially nesting birds of prey. *Power drills are illegal in Wilderness and all national parks.*

•**PARK AND CAMP IN DESIGNATED AREAS** Some climbing areas require a permit for overnight camping.

•**MAINTAIN A LOW PROFILE** Leave the boom box and day-glo clothing at home—the less climbers are heard and seen, the better.

•**RESPECT PRIVATE PROPERTY** Be courteous to land owners. Don't climb where you're not wanted.

•**JOIN THE ACCESS FUND** To become a member, make a tax-deductible donation of $35.

The Access Fund
*Keeping climbing areas open and
conserving the climbing environment*
PO Box 17010
Boulder, CO 80308 • 303.545.6772

**your climbing future
www.accessfund.org**

About the Coauthor:
Whipper

Whipper is a native Idahoan and a graduate of the school of barking at knocks. He was introduced to rock climbing in 1991 and quickly advanced to the 5.6 level. This achievement is especially remarkable considering the fact that he was born without opposable thumbs. Over the years, Whipper has been a fixture at the local crags and has made photo appearances in each of the "Boise Climbs" (and "Riggins Limestone") books. He is also well traveled, having visited (and "marked") dozens of climbing areas throughout the western United States. When he's not climbing, Whipper enjoys social sniffing, pettings from strangers and rolling in foul things. Now in his golden years, Whipper still gets out to the crags but these days prefers napping to climbing. One thing the passage of time has not changed is Whipper's legendary breath, which continues to turn heads (not to mention stomachs) and make quite a local stink.